Krzysztof Penderecki

LABYRINTH OF TIME

Five Addresses for the End of the Millennium

Hinshaw Music • Chapel Hill
1998

EDITOR
Ray Robinson

TRANSLATOR
William Brand

COVER DESIGN AND ILLUSTRATIONS
Ruth Robinson

TECHNICAL EDITOR
Darryl Miller

PHOTOGRAPH OF KRZYSZTOF PENDERECKI
Anne Osetek

Published by Hinshaw Music, Inc.,
P.O. Box 470, Chapel Hill, N.C. 27514

Library of Congress Catalog Card Number:
98-72403
ISBN: 0-937276-21-9

I am living just as the century ends.
A great leaf, that God and you and I
have covered with writing
turns now, overhead, in strange hands.
We feel the sweep of it like a wind.
We see the brightness of a new page
where everything yet can happen.

Unmoved by us, the fates take its measure
and look at one another, saying nothing.

Rainer Maria Rilke
From the *Book of Hours* (1899)

INTRODUCTION

The fact that I was awarded several honorary doctorates in a short span of time prompted me to reflect on one current theme: the condition of the artist at the end of the century. I delivered addresses devoted to this idea at the universities that had distinguished me with their *honoris causa* titles: the Academy of Music in Cracow, the University of Warsaw, the Academy of Music in Warsaw, and the University of Glasgow. The last address was delivered in Munich as part of a series of lectures on The End of the Century.

It just so happened that I was preparing the Munich address at the same time that I was completing the composition of a work commissioned for the three–thousandth anniversary of Jerusalem. The involvement with the two projects simultaneously prompted the thought: What should we take along in the ark that will carry us into the next century? All people who regard themselves as part of the Judaeo–Christian tradition might ask themselves this same question.

In this book, I attempt to share my reflections and doubts about civilization. While trying to identify and name the symptoms of our *mal du siècle*, I have tried as far as possible to overcome the prevailing tone of pessimism. I have reached for various sources—historical and contemporary—and for current criticism, literature and art—in my effort to take the pulse of the times. Someone might object that there is too little music commentary in the book. However, it was my deliberate choice to interweave reflections about music with considerations of a more general nature.

The interview that I gave to Ray Robinson in New York is related to the topics of the addresses. This interview provided me with the occasion for additional personal reflections. I would like to thank Hinshaw Music, Inc., for taking the initiative in publishing *The Labyrinth of Time*, and the editors for their passion and the trouble they took over it.

April 1998 *Krzysztof Penderecki*

EDITOR'S NOTE

The desire to publish this short book of Penderecki's words grew out of the work of the Editorial Board of *Studies in Penderecki*, the scholarly journal on the life and music of the composer that was established in 1994 [Volume I was published in January 1998.]. A group of Penderecki scholars met in the summer of 1994 to discuss ways by which research in the composer's music could be coordinated on a world wide basis. The result was the resolve to disseminate information of this type in the English language through traditional publications and electronic means. *Labyrinth of Time*, which reveals important aspects of Penderecki's compositional philosopy and his thoughts on the state of the musical art at the end of the century, is the most recent effort in the fulfillment of this goal.

Since 1970, more than thirty doctoral studies have been completed on the composer's life and works. The essays, which are the primary content of this volume, only add to the fascination with this original voice from Poland. Each of these addresses was written as a response to a specific honor which the composer received in the last decade of the century. Their published sources are listed below:

I. Address delivered on receipt of the title of Doctor *honoris causa* of the University of Warsaw, December 21, 1993. The Polish version was first published in *Tygodnik Powszechny* nr 1 (1994), p. 10.

II. Address given on the receipt of the title of Doctor *honoris causa* of the Academy of Music in Cracow, October 15, 1994. The Polish version was first published in *Plus Minus*, a supplement to *Rzeczpospolita* nr 43 (October 29–30, 1994), p. 14. An English version of this lecture was published in *Studies in Penderecki* 1:1 (1998), p. 9–11.

III. Address delivered on the receipt of the title of Doctor *honoris causa* of the Academy of Music in Warsaw, December 14, 1994. The Polish version was first published in *Plus Minus*, a supplement to *Rzeczpospolita* nr 52 (December 31, 1994 – January 1, 1995), p. 14.

IV. Address given on receipt of the title of Doctor *honoris causa* of the University of Glasgow, December 2, 1995. The Polish version was first published in *Plus Minus*, a supplement to *Rzeczpospolita* nr 48 (December 2–3, 1995), p. 14.

V. Address delivered at the Residenztheater in Munich, Germany, on December 18, 1996, to open the "End of the Century" cycle. The Polish version was first published in *Plus Minus*, a supplement to I 52 (December 22–26, 1996), p. 9–11.

May 1, 1998 Ray Robinson

TABLE OF CONTENTS

LABYRINTH OF TIME

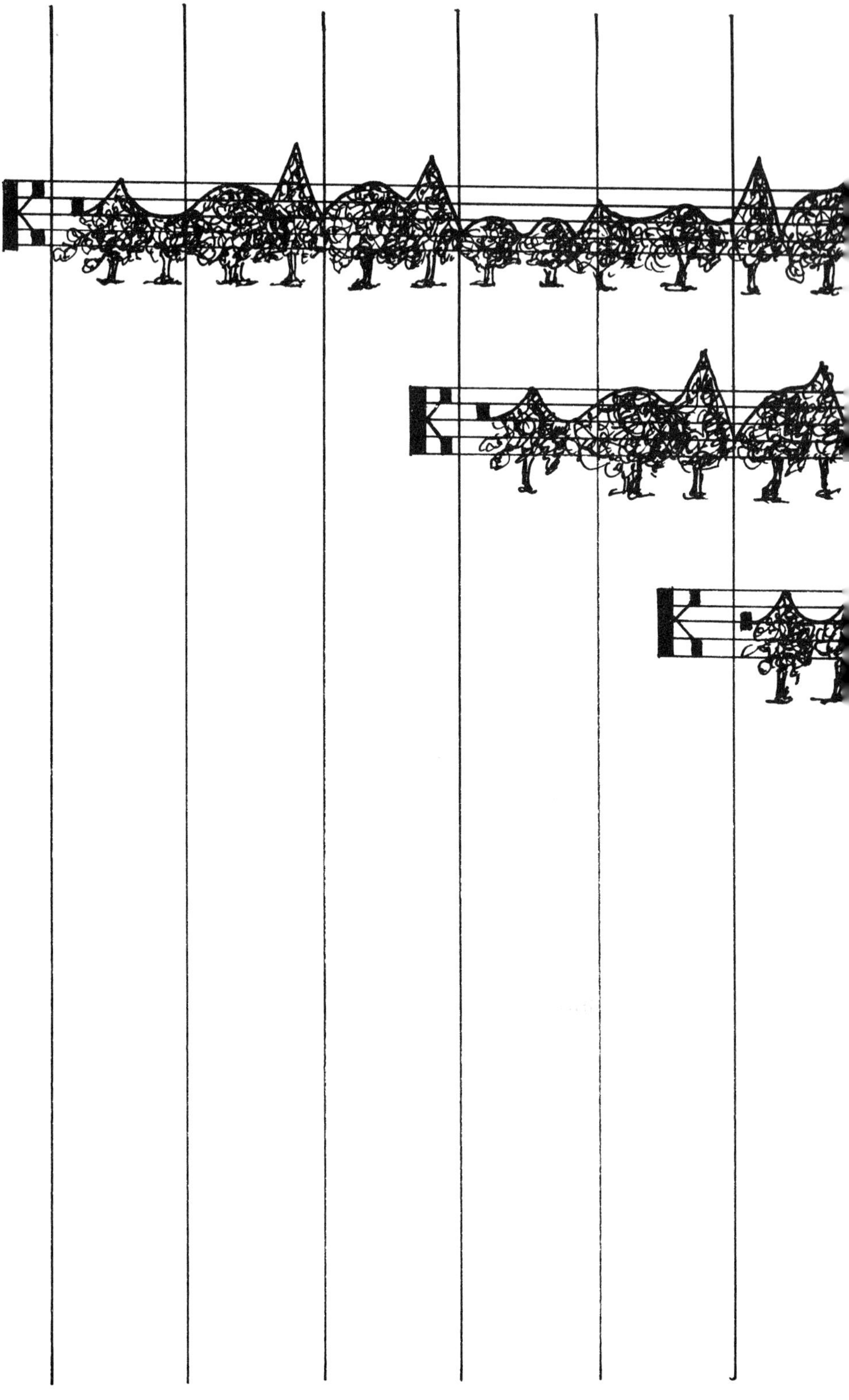

I

THE TREE INSIDE

The outstanding political commentator and critic Julian Klaczko said, paraphrasing Goethe, that "just as in literature, so also in the life–story of every eminent human being, we can see the epoch of the Iliad and the epoch of the Odyssey." The first is the "period of youthful heroism," "the epic of struggle," and the second is the "period of manliness and the search for the return," the "epic of tired age and nostalgia for home."[1]

I also have my Iliad and my Odyssey. For me, Troy was the avant–garde, the era of youthful rebellion and faith in the possibility of changing the way of the world through art. The avant–garde offered the illusion of universality. We young composers—hampered by the aesthetics of socialist realism that prevailed in Poland—regarded the musical world of Stockhausen, Nono, Boulez and Cage as liberation. I began my career at a time when there was still much left to discover. A new vision of art and the world, were opening before me. Quickly, however, I realized that there was more of destruction than of building anew in the innovation that boiled down mainly to formal experiments and speculation; the Promethean tone of those days was a utopia. The escape from the avant–garde trap of formalism enabled me to turn back towards tradition. I was even called "the Trojan horse of the avant– garde." Not until *Cosmogony,* at the beginning of the seventies, however, did I manage to free myself of that utopian faith in the possibility of building "one great family of man," which was an equally important element in the avant–garde doctrine.

Of course, it was hardly my intention—even as I sought inspiration in tradition—to become a traditionalist. I can identify with the words that Joseph addresses to Amenhotep IV in Thomas Mann's novel:

> The example of tradition comes from the depths, from what lies at the bottom, and that is what binds us together. But the 'I' comes from God, and appertains to a spirit that is free.[2]

This is the moment where my Ulyssean adventure begins, which "through travails, dangers and pain travels towards the lost Ithaca," my Odyssey, in other words, the creation of my own way, the search for the center.

I was guided by a longing for synthesis, a desire to integrate the welter of experience that is the lot of contemporary man. Each past age has left behind its own recognizable language. Bach or Mozart knew for whom they were writing, and knew that they would be understood. The contemporary artist, despite his longing for universality, is fragmented and alienated. For me, the conscious use of tradition became an opportunity for overcoming this dissonance between the artist and the audience. I look back feelingly on my *Passion According to St. Luke*, which constituted a turning point in my artistic journey. I reached for the archetype of the Passion—and thus for a theme 2,000 years old—in order to express not only the sufferings and death of Christ, but also the cruelty of our own century, the martyrdom of Auschwitz... and, today, I would add: the martyrdom of Sarajevo. I wanted the spectator to be drawn by the tension and drama of the music into the very heart of what was happening—as in a medieval mystery play, at which no one viewed it from a distance. Each spectator can be drawn into that *Passion* crowd, the *turba*, which demands that Christ be crucified. Similarly, each spectator finds salvation. The old theme was brought up to date by new means of expression.

Malicious critics accused me of eclecticism, which was the opposite of what I had intended. Synthesis cannot depend on the mechanical connecting of elements, but must rather be a homogenous alloy resulting from a unifying experience. I do not deny that I always felt tempted by many styles. Polystylistics—so fashionable now—was already present in the *Passion* and Matins [*Utrenya*], not to speak of my more recent works, such as *The Black Mask* and *King Ubu*, which result, each in their own way, from the deliberately accepted aesthetics of post–modernism. I am a hybrid. My family comes from the Eastern Marches of Poland. My paternal grandmother was Armenian, and my grandfather German. I have always felt, for example, attracted to Orthodox liturgy, while at the same time being fascinated by Western culture and its rationalism, and also by its capacity for expressing the most complex states and feelings. After all, Mediterranean culture—which is my home in the broadest of senses—arose precisely out of that fruitful linking of the most varied elements and influences.

I feel within myself the need for variety, and some ascribe to me the traits of the mythical Proteus, who kept constantly changing his appearance. The acute critic will perceive an inherent logic here. I am tempted by both the *sacrum* and the *profanum,* God and the devil, the sublime and its violation. Sublime works of the *sacra rappresentatione* type must find their counterpoint in iconoclastic or buffo forms. I cannot be sure that I have not sinned too much, especially towards the free "I," in yielding to the imperatives of power and the national ethos. Works like the *Polish Requiem,* or the earlier *Threnody for the Victims of Hiroshima,* while they may possess an autonomous artistic existence, are liable to be read as journalism. I fear the mixing of orders; I would not want that music, written in particular times, to be background for something else, subject to the same simplification.

Today, after passing through a lesson in late romanticism and utilizing the possibilities of post–modernistic thinking, I see my artistic ideal in claritas. I am returning to chamber music, for I realize that more can be said in a hushed voice condensed in the sound of three or four instruments. That escape into musical privacy is its own sort of answer to our *fin de siècle,* this speeding up of the historical clock, this confusion associated with the reshuffling of the norms in culture, ethics and politics. Might not this escape from a world turning sour, this surrounding oneself with the wall of a *cordon sanitaire,* not be desertion, some sort of symptom of a new Biedermeier? *Musica domestica* instead of great oratorios involved in the renewal of the world, planting trees instead of struggle and conquest?

My attitude is best defined by the words of a poet of the last *fin de siècle,* Rainer Maria Rilke:

And I, who want to grow,
Look inside, and in me grows a tree.[3]

The alchemists supposed that the perfection of the self must be accompanied by the regeneration of nature. Planting trees in Lusławice, where I have found the haven of my Odyssey, my Ithaca, I feel as if I am purifying myself, approaching the essence of myself and the essence of music. According to the esoteric teachings, that *materia prima* of which the alchemists built their *Opus Magnum* was accessible through inquiry into nature. Seeking the most concentrated and economical of forms, I too am thinking of such a synthesis. It is precisely chamber music that is the source of the approach to the *materia prima* of music for me. Will this stage lead me to the anticipated Grand Synthesis, the *Opus Magnum*? It seems to me that the recovery of the genuine and natural, the universal language of music, is possible only through such a purification and transmutation of everything that already exists.

II

THE ARTIST IN THE LABYRINTH

> Only one thing matters to me, whether I am approaching it slowly, in a roundabout way, inching this way or that, getting farther away, returning. I am always drawing nearer to the same goal. Approaching what? Approaching knowledge, although I do not know what kind, approaching balance and understanding,

wrote Czesław Miłosz in his book *The Unattainable Earth*.[4] He expressed the general human situation, and particularly that of the artist at the end of the century. We find ourselves in a labyrinth. We start down many paths, we back up and return with a highly unclear sense of our objective. We want to draw up a reckoning, to understand not only the individual path, but also that of the whole century that is drawing to a close. However, I fear that it is impossible to do so at the moment.

Italo Calvino expressed this impossibility most tellingly in one of his five *American Lectures*:

> I sometimes have the impression that some sort of epidemic has come over humanity, striking at its most characteristic property—speech: a kind of linguistic plague that presents itself as a loss of the powers of cognition and directness, a tendency to the automatic limitation of the means of expression, to the most general, anonymous, abstract formulations, to the erasure of significance, the dulling of the edge of expression, the extinguishing of each spark that flies from the striking of words against a new context."[5]

Our predecessors from the last *fin de siècle* obviously had this same feeling that language is inadequate to reality. Yet we are in a worse situation. One hundred years ago, art had a pre–eminently individualistic quality; today, we find ourselves in thrall to a bland mass culture.

In the same essay on "Exactness," Calvino wrote:

> We are immersed in an uninterrupted flow of images; the ubiquitous media constantly only transform the world into images and copy it through a phantasmagoria of trick mirrors.... A large part of this cloud of images disperses instantaneously, like a dream, leaving nothing behind in memory. But the feeling of alienation and distaste is never dispersed."[6]

The dictates of the media dissolve everything into pap. Homogenized culture mixes levels, demolishes hierarchies, reduces the highbrow and the lowbrow to a sameness. In search of commercial success, managers serve up spiritual sustenance in ever more showy packages and combinations: renowned tenors sing popular arias unisono during sporting contests; the products of high technology—video cassettes and compact discs—replace the need for the first–hand experience of literature, film, theatre and music. It is the imagination that suffers most in this kaleidoscope of information. The crisis of imagination is our supreme problem.

To escape and close ourselves in our own world becomes a natural reflex. But can it rescue our creative powers? In Lusławice, I have surrounded my property, my garden, with a high wall in the belief—consonant with symbolic thought—that such a wall reinforces the inner forces growing there. Such a *hortus conclusus* is a world unto itself, my universe, with a harmony that I shape. Laying out rows of trees, putting down lawns and beds of flowers, I am aware of building my own Arcadia. I am also certain—like many of my predecessors—that I am devoting myself to "a virtuous and pleasant art."[7] Emulating earlier examples, I have also planted a maze, a labyrinth, in my garden. I feel sure of myself here; I know the ways in and the ways out; I have built it by the principles of *construzione legittima.*

Creativity and the real world form a different labyrinth. How can the artistic aim be achieved in this welter of roads, in this chaos in which we are living?

It may be some consolation that the labyrinth—a metaphor of our existence—is always a blend of irrational elements, of the unpredictable, with the predictable, which we can control. Only error and the roundabout way lead to fulfillment. *Nur der Umweg führt zur Volkommenheit,* suggests Gustav René Hocke, author of the classic book *Die Welt als Labyrinth.*[8] Looking at the twentieth century as a whole, we are more and more aware that precisely this intricate structure is the destiny of artists: Stravinsky, Schoenberg, Prokofiev, Picasso, Witkacy, Kantor. The last mentioned wrote:

> If development traditionally presents itself as a straight line, a spiral or concentric circles, then the graphic chart of my work would be a labyrinth. It is precisely the lack of a way out that shows that we are on the right track. In art, of course.[9]

We must therefore seek hope in paradoxes. The present situation of art does indeed suggest a dead–end. In all domains of art, we can see how ideas and materials are being used up; in music, the capacities of the instruments are being exploited. In my *Threnody* of 1960, the string instruments sound like percussion. Today, such a solution is nothing new. Despite the fact that we are drawing on so many sources of inspiration, from the accomplishments of the whole century, artistic language has become superficial and impoverished. We have reached a point where opening the door behind us is the summit of creativity. How far we have come from the artists of the first avant–garde, who had—even though this, too, proved a utopia—a clearly marked objective. We are more like those Baudelarian travellers, *qui partent pour partir*—who set out in order to set out.

But I don't want to fall into typical *fin de siècle* pessimism. Therefore I distance myself from Miłosz's image in his latest volume of *Facing the River*, no matter how beautiful it may be:

> That the gate of the Black Garden closes, peace, peace. What is finished is finished.[10]

I believe in neither the postmodernist "death of the author" nor in the "twilight of the great forms." I reject the currently fashionable effacement and disintegration of the structure of a work of art. Nor do I accept the victory of sophistry over imagination. It is necessary to have a keen intelligence and consciousness, but also to listen intently to one's inner world. As it was formulated so insightfully by the Israeli writer Amos Oz:

> When a man sits down in order, let us say, to compose, he must on the one hand be aware and have senses as sharp as an assassin in a 'Night of the Long Knives,' when every moment can turn out to be critical, and on the other, he must be enraptured as in a dream. If he is only alert, he will not create a work of art. Nor will any music arise if he is totally enraptured in that dream.[11]

One must have the courage to be oneself. The period of stagnation, the wearing away of individual characteristics in art, cannot last forever. Art must be reborn. I am no seer. I shall not prophesy about the pictures that painters will paint or the way the music of the future will sound. Yet I believe in a future avant–garde, understood not as an institution (we all know that it was precisely institutionalization that compromised the avant–garde movement in our century), but rather as the heart of genuine creativity.

"And who will act as the forward guard ahead of me?" asks Charlemagne in the *Song of Roland.* That question about the forward guard, about the avant–garde, is still relevant.

III

THE END OF THE CENTURY DOES NOT MEAN THE END OF ART

In his famous 1912 tract *On the Spiritual in Art*, Wassily Kandinsky compared the scheme of the spiritual life to a great triangle divided into unqual parts.[12] The sharp, upward–pointing summit symbolizes full spirituality. Below, nearer the wide base, there is less of that element of spirituality, and it is more diffused. Artists can be found in each of these parts, but there are fewer of them, at times only one, at the summit. The whole triangle is rising almost imperceptibly. Much time will have to pass, however, before the base reaches the level where the summit once stood, and before the vision of that solo artist becomes a common possession. Kandinsky found an example in the genius—untimely solitary—of Beethoven, who was not acknowledged and revered until the generation of the modernists, including Kandinsky himself, came along. Today—and this is something that no one could then have predicted—Beethoven has, like, so many other classics, been appropriated by mass culture. A supreme value has landed in the lowest regions.

As difficult as is is to identify a coherent set of characteristics of the contemporary epoch, there can be no doubt about one such characteristic. Never before has mass culture—populism—had such significance as at present, in a negative sense, of course. This phenomenon has a relatively recent lineage. It appeared after the French Revolution, along with democratic social relations and the development of universal education. As the eminent British sociologist Dwight MacDonald states,

> mass culture is a dynamic, revolutionary force that demolishes the barriers of class, tradition and taste while obliterating cultural differences.... Mass culture is very, very democratic: it characteristically rejects discrimination against anyone, between anyone and anything. Everything is grist for its mill, and comes out of that mill ground smooth.[13]

It is hardly strange that the canon of that culture, in contradistinction to culture tout court, derives from the most democratic country in the world, the United States. Nor it is strange that the most vital reaction against populism has now arisen in that same country. In a book that has recently provoked much discussion, *In Defense of Elitism*, the two–time Pulitzer prize winner and critic William A. Henry III casts a veto against the abuse of the popular policy of multiculturalism in his country, while questioning the American myth of equality. "In the pursuit of egalitarianism," he writes,

> an ideal rapidly diverging from the way it was understood by the Founding Fathers, we have deliberately blinded ourselves to the elementary truth . . . that some people are better than others—they are faster, work harder, learn bet-

> ter, are more productive and more irreplaceable. Some ideas are better than others, some values are more enduring, some works of art are more universal. Some cultures—though we dare not say so—are richer than others, and thus more worthy of esteem. Every corner of the earth where people live has something to offer. But this does not mean that all the shares are equal.[14]

The disease of populism seems even more dangerous in Poland, because we lack defensive mechanisms. The superstition that acknowledges the correctness and superiority of the tastes of the majority emerges in particularly drastic form in a poor country degraded by totalitarianism. Let us recall, in the words of Józef Bocheński, author of the brilliant book *Sto zabobonów* (One Hundred Superstitions), what the true èlite is:

> The true èlite is the same as the generality of the most outstanding people in a given society—the most outstanding in terms of character, knowledge, intelligence, creative ability, and so on. In this meaning, the èlite is the opposite of the mass.[15]

Bocheński warns that yielding to the superstition being spread today about the uselessness of the èlite involves grave risks to society:

> This is because the prosperity, progress and at times even the very survival of a society depend on whether it is capable of creating a good èlite—writes the philosopher—a society without an èlite is doomed to petrifaction and sudden death.[16]

This diagnosis fits Poland exactly: our society, lacking the backbone of authorities, resembles a sponge capable of soaking up all that is worst. In such a country, it is highly difficult to create authentic values, while it is shockingly easy to squander and destroy them. A shocking example can be found in the liquidation of the renowned Radio Orchestra in Cracow, or in the predicament of opera companies. The lack of money is an alibi for the destruction of authentic phenomena and talents, and a rationalization for stagnation and inertia.

The general atmosphere of decadence only exacerbates the problem. To return to Kandinsky, we can use his description of epochs like ours:

> In the world of the spirit, there are sterile periods, poor in talent, where no one provides people with the bread of illumination. These are the periods of decadence. Souls fall continually into the nether regions of the triangle, which seems as a whole to be immobilized. In reality, however, it is withdrawing and sinking. In these dumb epochs, where the vision is clouded and turned towards darkness, people acknowledge particularly, almost exclusively, the values of external success. Only material goods count; each technical advance that can serve no other end than the body is heralded as a triumph. Purely spiritual forces pass by unobserved.[17]

What is more, the time in which we live cannot even be called vulgar, since the very concept has lost its eloquence. In the meantime, vulgarization penetrates all areas of life, from politics to art. King Ubu is enjoying a renaissance as the patron of presidents. We are drifting into the unknown on a ship of fools. Contemporary people, desirous of filling the void, seek ever stronger stimuli in the multimedia substrata, thanks to the new technology. Scholars threaten us with the vision of *homo pyknolepticus*, who, overwhelmed by a surfeit of attractions, becomes incapable of thinking.[18] History has not the slightest intention of concluding before our eyes with an Arcadian happy ending, as proclaimed several years ago by the over–advertised Fukuyama. Rather, it will assume ever more shocking forms, at times grotesque and at times monstrous. Zbigniew Herbert brilliantly expressed this "festival of the apocalypse" in his poem "Babylon":

> This is the end of the world fully laden Etruscan tables they are celebrating unaware of fate shirts stained with wine in the end the barbarians come to slash the aorta.[19]

Does this mean that the universal catastrophe, foretold all through the twentieth century, is to come to pass? I am increasingly aware that I have apocalyptic tendencies—that means that the vision of the ultimate crash hardly paralyzes me, but rather activates and sets free my powers. In this, I can identify with Kandinsky himself and the kindred artists who formed the avant–garde at the turn of the century, and who liberated new creative energies of their own in the face of the unavoidable catastrophe. Of course, I do not share their millenarianism. They lived by the apocalypse, seeking its signs, believing that it would be followed by a grand transformation of life and art, an epoch of great spirituality. I have no ambitions to right the world's wrongs, and I am far from utopian thinking. I am, however, convinced that our *fin de millênaire*, with its tonality of satiation and enervation, does not at all signify the end of art, the end of creativity. I have no doubts of the capacity of art for regeneration. In accordance with the natural rhythm of the change of generations, the eclectics of the present day will be succeeded by generations of modernists and renewers who will come on the scene like Count Roland's cohorts—with a battle cry of "Montjoie!"[20] Roland, the prototype of all avant–gardists, must die after taking up the unequal battle with the armies of the Saracens. He will, however, have set an example of determination and endless devotion to his vocation.

There is no artistic creation without that vocation, without internal necessity. Form must result from the crystallization of inwardly felt contents. This cannot be learned. There are no rules here. This is undeniably a gift. Czesław Miłosz began his Harvard lectures with this avowal:

> To speak forthrightly, I have been under the control of a demon all my life, and I do not really understand how the poems dictated by him came about.[21]

Witold Lutosławski put it similarly when he said, in perhaps the last of his interviews, that musical works are "emissaries from the ideal world."[22]

As long as that source of the sounds, images and words that flow to us does not run dry, as long as that "illumination taking shape in heaven," as Dante termed it, does not cease, then the capacity for creation will not become extinct, and the imagination will not perish.

IV

ELEGY FOR A DYING FOREST

It would be hard to think of a better definition of decadence than the one offered by Dostoyevsky. One of his novelistic protagonists says: it is "as if no one were ever to plant another tree."[23] One hundred years ago, it seemed that European culture had reached a zero point. Many symptoms show that the crisis of exhaustion of those times has since grown even worse.

Oswald Spengler, author of the notorious book *Der Untergang des Abendlandes* (The Decline of the West), compares a culture to an organism. Each culture—like a tree or a bird—has its time of birth, growth, maturity and decline. In the period of aging, as its vital forces dwindle, it turns into a civilization. A civilization is ossification, artificiality. A culture is nature.[24]

Much has been written about the mortality of the European culture that is most familiar to us. Believing personally that the mechanism of rebirth is permanently encoded in that culture, I still cannot fail to remark about the rapid tempo at which it is transforming itself into a civilization—in precisely the sense intended by Spengler.

The civilization of the end of the twentieth century, with its stunning technical progress, offers few reasons for optimism. The mass media feed us with information about emerging dangers. The apocalypse has become a newspaper story. Someone has even invented the term "sinistrose" to embrace all the forms of doubt, pessimism and nihilistic prophecies on the future of our world.[25]

Artists have lent their hands to the creation of this grim vision. Despite the prevailing eclecticism, one common tone is felt in the salons of renowned galleries, be they in London or in Warsaw.[26] At all costs, the art of the end of the century strives to stagger the beholder with its literalness and cruelty. Making use of the most up–to–date techniques, it shocks us with images of aggression, decay and death, bereft of all artistic refinement. And it is indeed difficult to identify artists capable of opposing the power of their art to these rituals of monstrosity and blandness.

One such artist was undoubtedly my illustrious countryman Tadeusz Kantor, who showed in his extraordinary "theatre of the emotions" how to defend the autonomy of the imagination against the furor of our times. In his *Twelfth Milano Lesson* (1986), regarded as a manifesto of the end of the twentieth century, the artist warns us against the plagues of civilization, which increasingly subordinate individual creativity to "The Omnipotent Art Market and Holy Commerce." The supreme threat is "Omnipotent Holy Technology," which leads to idolatry and pseudo–creativity. In an almost prophetic vein, Kantor writes:

Among those false
Priests of Trade and the Market
belong the gigantomaniacs,
thoughtless calculators,
who with unusual cunning
arrange for their ends
the grandness of nature,
mountain chains,
desert sands, which
they cover with paint,
sculpt with bulldozers,
anything to be visible
in the world's shop window.[27]

Technology also makes possible the facile production of art in the spirit of the New Age, which is fodder for mass culture. How well we know these

SELF ASSURED MAKERS OF SPECTACLES,
OVERLY CAPRICIOUS PSEUDO–POETS,
FAKERS TRYING TO ENTHRALL US WITH THEIR HYSTERIA,
WHOSE MEDIOCRE IMAGINATIONS ARE SALVAGED BY TECHNOLOGY
AND ITS ULTRAMECHANISMS,
EXTERMINATING WITHOUT SCRUPLE
THE MIND AND EMOTIONS.[28]

Cheap spiritualism has become a trait of the end of our century. It replaces authentic spirituality, which man—announcing the "Death of God"—has expelled from his world. This is one more characteristic of civilization as Spengler understood it.

The desacralization of nature goes hand in hand with

the desacralization of standards, manners and artistic creation. Never before has the Faustian passion for destruction run to such extremes. In an essay with the eloquent title *The Tree without Gods*, the Italian writer Guido Ceronetti observes,

> If a cedar of Lebanon, older than the pyramids, growing in the courtyard of some building, should happen to hinder eleven lawyers, nine merchants, three dentists, a photographer and a pediatrician in parking their cars, then they cut it down without a moment's hesitation. However, were there to exist a prophecy that the whole building would crumble to dust after the cedar of Lebanon is felled, because killing the tree would also kill the protective spirit of the place, then respect and fear would have the upper hand and no one would dare lift their hand to cut down the tree.[29]

Nature, nevertheless, is only dead material, devoid of transcendental associations, for people who have lost the habit of holiness. Ecological rationalism can be of little aid here. The death of trees, woods and tropical rain forests is more than a biological problem. The culture that sins against the forests cuts off its own reason for being. Thus have we created a civilization that—as Ehrenfried Pfeiffer so vividly defined it in *The Ecologist*—"has processed sixty thousand years of evolution into wrapping paper."[30]

It is not clear whether Beethoven, were he alive today, would write the Pastoral Symphony. If so, it would not be the same. The musical portrait of nature would have to sound different. I myself, should I manage to compose my sixth symphony, will title it "Elegy for a Dying Forest."

And yet I have decided to "conclude a pact of happiness with nature." And, despite what Dostoyevsky's hero suggests, I am planting trees. In my country residence at Lusławice, situated among the rolling hills of southern Poland, I have laid out an arboretum. During the last twenty years, I have collected more than 1500 species of trees there. I planted each one myself. Composing the garden has, for me, much in common with composing a musical work. In the one as in the other, what counts is the constructive imagination, the ability to think of the whole. A garden is, after all, nature mathematized, just as music is emotion mathematized. I must say, indeed, that I feel far more sure of myself as a dendrologist than as a composer. I cannot think of another period in the history of music as marked by decline as our own. No new paths of development can be seen. Artists are exploiting old ideas and turning back into the past.

Is it really necessary, however, to fear going back? After all, it was Apollinaire himself who, in the youth of our century, pointed out that

> no matter how far the search for freedom leads, it will only cause the strengthening of traditional rules and the rise of new rules, which will be no less rigorous than the old ones.[31]

Look at a tree. It teaches us that a work of art must be doubly rooted: in the earth and in the air. No creation can come about without roots.

That is why I have taken the risk of my own *regressus ad uterum.* Ethnologists assure us that such a return backwards, to the sources, can have a revitalizing force.[32] At work these days on the composition of a work for the three–thousandth anniversary of Jerusalem [*The Seven Gates of Jerusalem*], I have decided to return to the *Psalms of David*. This is a multiple return: to the roots of Judaeo–Christian culture, to the sources of music, and, finally, to the beginnings of my own work. I first reached out to that archetypal pattern of our culture in a youthful composition. Entering upon the path of avant–garde art, I had the presentiment that one cannot cut oneself off from one's spiritual roots. I chose four Psalms that are cries to God. Today, almost forty years later, I can see more clearly that only the *homo religiosus* can count on salvation.

That promise is like the tree planted at the beginning of the Book of Psalms:

> *Blessed is the man that walketh not in the counsel of the ungodly, nor standeth in the way of sinners, nor sitteth in the seat of the scornful.*
>
> *But his delight is in the law of the Lord: and in his law doth he meditate day and night.*
>
> *And he shall be like a tree planted by the rivers of water, that bringeth forth his fruit in his season: his leaf also shall not wither: and whatsoever he doeth shall prosper.*
>
> *Psalm* 1, 1–3[33]

V

THE ARK

I

> Times of decline and fall also have a sacred right
> to our sympathy,[34]

wrote Jakob Burckhardt in his reflections on the sense of history. We do not know whether the great scholar would also have applied his words to our era, but they are worth recalling particularly at present, when we are simply being deluged with gloomy diagnoses and dark forecasts. It is obviously not easy to perceive foreshadowings of a turning point in times of crisis—yet I suppose that the sympathy shown to difficult times must depend on precisely such foreshadowings. The love of future generations—the Greek *storge*—nevertheless obliges us to believe that genes of unending renewal are coded into the human species.

Storge was a favorite word of Oskar Miłosz,[35] a little–known poet and visionary who died in 1939. While experiencing the tragedy of his times, he was capable of maintaining a positive distance. In his poetic tract *Ars Magna*, published in Paris in 1924, he wrote,

> Need I add that the age in which I have suffered as no mortal heart ever suffered, is the stupidest and most abject of all, an age of movement in all fields, in love, in art, in science, in politics?... And yet I love and admire my age, and I thank my Master for having thrown me into it: an excess of movement is, after all, a process of decay and the source of new life."[36]

Directing those words to the reader of the future, to his "spiritual posthumous grandchildren," Miłosz specified the way to understand that dual sense of the movement, of confusion, decay and the *Turba Magna*:

> because our great political and social wars are terrible plows, our conception of love is fertilizer, and our science is the softened grain that has not yet begun to sprout under the sun of renewal."[37]

Oskar Miłosz, a Lithuanian aristocrat living in Paris, is numbered among the most esoteric poets in the French language. He belonged to a family of *grands initiés*, the "great initiated." Solitary by choice, he compensated for his "turning away from life" with a prophetic attitude. He anticipated the coming of a great renewal, his beloved Re–naissance. Although reality filled him with "shivers of extraordinary aversion," he believed in spiritual progress. He tried to rethink the place of the transcendental in a world that denied the existence of the transcendental. As the British researcher into his philosophy, Philip Sherard, writes, Oskar Miłosz also tried to reconsider the situation of man "ejected into a kind of infernal void."[38]

We see in Oskar Miłosz the tension typical of utopian

thought. Criticism of the status quo finds its necessary fulfillment in the prophetic vision of rebirth. It is amazing how far we are today from similar thinking. There can be no doubt that our mistrust of utopia stems from the experience of the twentieth century, which turns out to have been the century of applied utopianism. "And thus Marxism is not utopia per se, but something new: an applied utopia,"[39] states Ernst Bloch in a book with the significant title *Abschied von der Utopie?* (Farewell to Utopia?). Many of the intellectuals of our century have tried—and are still trying—to think through the traumatic experience of the applied utopia, in the totalitarian version, to which three generations were subjected: our parents, we ourselves, and our children.

It is characteristic, however, that in rejecting totalitarianism, we have in general jettisoned thinking in categories of goals. Whatever happened to the idea of progress, which was immanent in our civilization? I recently read an interesting dialogue in a French magazine. It stated that the concept of progress has been superseded at present by two interconnected concepts: communication and the market.[40] To be accurate, one must add that these concepts lie at the foundations of European culture. Inquiring into the origins of Europe in a 1922 lecture at the university of Zurich, Paul Valéry postulated that Europe arose in the Mediterranean basin out of the exchange of spiritual and material goods. The Mediterraneum was the great market where pre–European communication was carried out. The poet says,

> This triumphant Europe, which was born in such a small territory...reminds me of a bustling marketplace to which everything noble

> and precious was brought to be discussed and exchanged from hand to hand. It is a market where the most varied doctrines, ideas, and discoveries are offered for sale and assessed. They are the object of merciless criticism and equally blind praise; their prices rise and fall.[41]

Let us examine the dynamics of this exchange and the risk, seriousness, and involvement associated with it.

Today, as the Naples–based Polish writer Gustaw Herling–Grudziński observes, Europe rather resembles "the miserable remnants of the ex–navel of the world." The quality of what we exchange is thought–provoking. Our communication has lost its subject. It is hard to ignore the symptoms of "information overflow." I would like to refer here to the views of George Steiner, the British literary scholar with Central–European roots, who has become one of the major critics of the "post–verbal" epoch. Steiner opposes the linguistic chaos of our time, which is caused by the expansion of the mass–media culture and the regression of the culture of the word. His well–known essay *The Broken Contract* begins with the assertion that: "It is possible to say everything, and therefore to write about everything."[42] Language has been removed beyond the bounds of good and evil. The contract that served as the foundation of Hebrew and Greek culture has been broken. It rested on the guarantee of "authentic presence," on the belief that the word corresponds to objective reality.

It is precisely that breaking of the covenant between words and the world that constitutes one of the few spiritual revolutions in the history of the West, and that defines the contemporary world,[43] writes Steiner. Another

Central European who holds a chair at an American university, Czesław Miłosz, formulates his diagnosis in a similar style. In his introduction to the writings of his uncle, the above–mentioned Oskar Miłosz, the Nobel–prize–winning poet states that the central characteristics of our splendid age are annihilation and "the replacement of drama by indifference":

> Despair, screams, accusations against God, asking questions about the origins of Evil—all of this has fallen silent. The issues with which man wrestled for millennia have been reduced to the vagaries of language, and the concepts of truth or falsehood have been banished."[44]

It is therefore also curious to observe the optimism of the residents of the "global village," the users of the new computer and mass–media technologies, who believe themselves to have achieved full communication—like the communication of the angels. As Hartmut Böhme writes in his sketch *Zur Theologie der Telepräsenz* (On the Theology of the Telepresence"),

> the 'global village' feeds on religious ideas. It assumes that, off to the side, or above a world full of contradictions, it is possible to build a telematic world in which the act of communication leads to the communion of the participants in communication. (We are all such participants.) In the 'global village' we all, like angels, are interconnected, we interact with each other, we are all equal, open and authentic, we understand each other perfectly and keep each other mutually informed, creating a society that

> is communicative beyond time and space, no,
> an almost pre–communist society."[45]

The myth of universal communication in a particularly radical version—the *linguae angelorum*—has come alive. But instead of a telematic paradise, we are rather living the drama of the inadequacy of language to the world of our experiences.

> (. . .) too few strings
> a choir needed
> a sea of laments
> a thunder of mountains
> a rain of stones
>
> (. . .) what way out
> of the human ruin
> what way out
> of the choir's verses—(. . .)[46]

wrote Zbigniew Herbert in his poem "Troy". These words about the impotence of poetry were written by one of the greatest poets working in my language.

> (. . .) the poet wrestles with his own shadow
> the poet cries like a bird in the desert
>
> (. . .) the poet's silence rain falls.[47]

II

I have long been thinking about the deluge and the necessity of building an ark. Yahweh may indeed have concluded a New Covenant with man at the end of the Biblical cataclysm and promised that "neither shall there any more be a flood to destroy the earth" (Genesis 9, 11). Times like ours, nevertheless, encourage a return to that primal myth of the flood.

I would not wish to be suspected here of decadence or of crying, in the spirit of the modernists of a century ago: *Après nous le déluge*. However, I cannot agree with Joseph Brodsky, the great Russian poet who died not long ago in New York, who wrote in *Fin de siècle*, as if he were mocking that note:

> After us no annihilation
> —an oar will suffice for the flood —.[48]

I am afraid that an oar will not suffice to get us out of the "apocalypse of fluidity" that is reaching its tidal crest now, at the end of the century and the millennium. I wonder, therefore, how the new ark should be built.

The symbol of the ark is one of the most richly significant in the Judaeo–Christian tradition. In Hebrew, *aron* means a case, a chest, a box. And therefore the ark—as the dictionary of Biblical symbols informs us—is a box of enormous dimensions, more a floating house than a ship, with a capacity for many beings, both human and animal.[49] Yahweh, seeing iniquity spread on earth, decided to obliterate what He had created. He offered salvation only to the righteous: Noah and his family. We read in the Book of Genesis:

> *And God looked upon the earth, and, behold, it was corrupt; for all flesh had corrupted his way upon the earth.*
>
> *And God said unto Noah, The end of all flesh is come before me; for the earth is filled with violence through them; and behold, I will destroy them with the earth.*
>
> *Genesis* 6, 12–13

Then comes the exact description of how Noah is supposed to construct the ark:

> *Make thee an ark of gopher wood; rooms shalt thou make in the ark, and shalt pitch it within and without with pitch. And this is the fashion which thou shalt make it of: the length of the ark shall be three hundred cubits, the breadth of it fifty cubits, and the height of it thirty cubits.*
>
> *A window shalt thou make to the ark, and in a cubit shalt thou finish it above; and the door of the ark shalt thou set in the side thereof; with lower, second and third stories shalt thou make it.*
>
> *Genesis* 6, 14–16

Who should go into the ark was also specified. Yahweh said:

> *But with thee will I establish my covenant; and thou shalt come into the ark, thou, and thy sons, and thy wife, and thy sons' wives with thee. And of every living thing of all flesh, two of every sort shalt thou bring into the ark, to keep them alive with thee, they shall be male and female.*

> *Of fowls after their kind, and of cattle after their kind, and of every creeping thing of the earth after his kind, two of every sort shall come unto thee, to keep them alive*
>
> *Genesis* 6, 18–20

Despite his intention of destroying the whole earth, God nevertheless decided to preserve the seeds of future life in the ark, "to keep seed alive upon the face of all the earth" (Genesis 7, 3). Ethnologists have shown that all flood myths have the same symbolism: they speak of the necessity of utterly annihilating the depraved world and humanity, in order to make possible a new creation—in other words, to restore its primal integrity. The ark is therefore compared to a seed floating on the surface of the water. In it are preserved all the necessary elements of the future cosmogony.

In time, the Biblical ark—so real in its construction that it could become the paradigm for the architecture of the future—was supplanted in imagination by the mystical ark. Examples may be found in the theological tracts of late antiquity and the medieval period: *De Noe et arca* by the Church Father, St. Ambrose, or two tracts by Hugo of St. Victor, *De arca Noe morali* and *De arca mystica.* Both compare Noah's Ark to the human body, with its limbs and, especially, its heart. They thus suggest, I suppose, that everyone carries his own salvation, his own ark, inside.

The ultimate updating of the theme of the flood and Noah's Ark is to be found in a sermon preached by Hieronymous Savonarola in the cathedral of Florence in 1494. This was an especially dramatic period of political upheaval and transformation during the passage from the medieval to modern times. Anticipation of the year 1500 was almost hysterical. Christ's Second Coming and the end of the world were expected. The inspired monk from the Monastery of San Marco, who for two years won the obedience of all Florence, enunciated the necessity of a moral renewal and conversion, since an irrevocable sentence of annihilation hung over the Church and Italy, "over the profaned garden of God." Savonarola preached two cycles of sermons in 1494, his *Prediche sopra l'arca di Noe*—44 Lenten sermons and 13 Advent sermons. I have held in my hands the 1536 Florence edition of the Advent sermons,[50] and I saw how concretely this prophet of modern times thought about the construction of the spiritual ark. Just as in the Book of Genesis, he describes its construction and its internal divisions. Instead of animals, however, it is to be filled with the noblest representatives of all classes.

Savonarola, like Noah, wanted to save a select community from the coming deluge. From this remnant, after the cessation of the catastrophe, a new cycle of history would begin: *il nuovo giro.*

As we know, the monk's plans ended in defeat. In 1498—500 years ago—he was himself burned at the stake, but his voice resounds even today as an admonition. I thought of Savonarola while reading Gustaw Herling–Grudziński's most recent story, *Don Ildebrando*, where he writes of the contemporary delectation of evil, the *delectatio morbosa.* As he writes,

> It suffices to look around day after day, to read the newspapers, to watch television and films. Evil everywhere, growing, greedy, savage, clothed in delectation. . . . Evil has always pre-

> vailed, but it has never been so steeped in the element of the gratuitous—often, there is no reason for it at all. Evil for Evil's sake. It is not the delectation of Evil that is an aberration now, but the longing for Good.[51]

What can the artist do in this situation? One hundred years ago, it still seemed that art could be a means of salvation. Here in Munich, concepts were formulated which represented the fullest expression of the utopian belief in the renewing power of art. I am thinking of the theory and work of Wassily Kandinsky and the groupings of artists whom he led: the "Phalanx" (1901), the "Neue Künstlervereinigung–München" (1909), and, finally, the most important, "Der Blaue Reiter," which existed from 1911 until the outbreak of the First World War. There can be no doubt that the artists gathered around Kandinsky constituted one of the most creative assemblies of the time: in full consciousness of the transformation that was underway, they summed up the nineteenth century and opened wide perspectives for the art of our own century.

Kandinsky came to Munich in 1897, following other Russian artists who set the dominant tone in the international milieu of the Bavarian capital. What attracted them? Let us quote the views of Leonid Pasternak, a professor of the Moscow Academy of Fine Arts and the father of the great poet. Here is how he explained to his students the superiority of Munich over Paris:

> Paris is an agitated whirlwind, while Munich is a quiet, peaceful German city. It may be boring to some, but it is a very good place to study. It is possible to paint there, and that is the most important thing. That is the foundation.[52]

Kandinsky thus traveled to Munich in order to learn to paint. He was also attracted by the fairy–tale atmosphere that he found in this sleepy city, "surrounded by walls and deep moats." He must have had an amazingly strong presentiment of his own art, since he decided to begin his studies at the age of 31, abandoning a promising university career as a legal scholar in Russia.

Perhaps some of you saw the outstanding 1996 Kandinsky retrospective in the Lenbachhaus, *Das bunte Leben.*[53] That was a rare occasion to follow the artist's work, from his first academic sketches in the private studios of Anton Azby and Franz von Stuck, through the full realization of his vision. I was fascinated to trace the way that Kandinsky departed one by one from the conventions that were obligatory in his time: how he moved from academic realism to Art Nouveau; how the Art Nouveau fairyland of his engravings and paintings on glass coexists with the post–Impressionism of his early, tentative landscape painting; and how the confrontation with Fauvism and Expressionism finally hastens the emergence of a totally autonomous order of forms: the world of abstract painting.

It would be a mistake, however, to see in this artistic evolution merely a succession of formal transformations, or a purely external course of development. For Kandinsky, after all, the concept of forms was strictly connected with internal meanings, with the spiritual element that can be most fully expressed only through art—music, painting and poetry. Arnold Schoenberg joined the company of idealist painters who gathered around Kandinsky. Kandinsky commented on the great composer's painting:

> Decadence of form is decadence of the spirit, which means the decadence of significance.

> And the growth of the form is the growth of significance, which means, of the spirit.[54]

Only such a form could reach the beholder, evoking a filial vibration and contributing as a result to the beholder's spiritual transformation. Along this path towards the authentic living form, Kandinsky perceived three types of dangers which he himself had managed to bypass or reject. It is worth quoting the artist's admonitions, since they have a universal character. Each artist is threatened by:

1. the danger of stylized forms, forms that have died and been resuscitated or that are too weak to live;
2. the danger of ornamental forms which can essentially be reduced to external beauty, because they may be (and usually are) full of external expression while devoid of internal expression;
3. the danger of experimental forms, born of experiments and thus without the participation of the intuition, all the more so because every form possesses to some degree an internal content that falsely suggests an internal necessity.[55]

The most difficult thing is to recognize the authenticity or falsity of experimental forms. We should bear this in mind in our post avant–garde times.

III

Savonarola held that the condition for entering the spiritual ark is the attainment of a state of simplicity, since only *"ad nudam animam nudum verbum parveniat"* [sincerity of words comes from sincerity of the soul].[56] This ideal of primal simplicitatis is completely inaccessible to us. Are we therefore sentenced to eclecticism? A deluge would certainly be useful, to sweep up the old, exhausted forms, in order, as Mircea Eliade says, "to drown them finally in themselves, to cleanse them, to enrich them with new, hidden potential, and regenerate them."[57]

It is some consolation that we are not in a situation like that of one hundred years ago, when Paul Gauguin said, "In art there are only revolutionaries or plagiarists." We have gotten over the disease of revolution at all costs. The words of one of the founding fathers of the twentieth century avant–garde, Igor Stravinsky, are symptomatic. The distinguished Norton Lectures at Harvard in 1939 consisted of his cycle of addresses on *The Poetics of Music.* He said,

> I have been made into a revolutionary against my will. . . . Art is, in essence, constructive. Revolution, on the other hand, assumes the upsetting of equilibrium. To speak of revolution is to speak of momentary chaos. One does not sink into chaos without an immediate sense of danger both to one's actions and to one's very being."[58]

I am more and more conscious of the fact that in today's era of the dissolution of norms and values, our ark symbolizes precisely the feeling of examples and measures, the designation of one's own borders, without which it is impossible to create any work of art—in spite of the philosophy of incapacity as propounded by the adherents of post–modernism.

Such an ark of values was laid out in literature by Italo Calvino, the Italian writer, prematurely deceased in 1985, who prepared erudite and prophetic talks, regarded as masterpieces of the essay, for those same Norton Lectures at Harvard. Critics have referred to Italo Calvino's *American Lectures* as a testament of twentieth–century literature.[59] Calvino never managed to finish or to deliver them.

What particular literary attributes does Calvino recommend to the coming millennium? The writer is aware, with all his insight, of the threats to the art of the word in an age of acquired illiteracy brought about by the development of the post–industrial culture of the image. His confidence in the future of literature is admirable. It stems, he writes,

> from the conviction that things exist which can be communicated only by literature, through the intermediacy of the means of expression proper to it.

These properties—which, in my opinion, are shared by music—were the subjects of Calvino's subsequent essays: Lightness, Quickness, Exactitude, Clarity, Variety. It is symbolic that he did not manage to write the last essay, titled Coherence. An Italian critic associated with the trans avant–garde, Achille Bonito Oliva, states that precisely the lack of coherence—"the irreducibility of each fragment combined with an inability to create integrity and balance"[60]—is the dominant characteristic of our times.

Is this incoherence truly insuperable? Drawing yet another analogy with the preceding *fin de siècle*, one can still maintain hope. With a similar state of awareness, artists emerged then who were capable of processing the sense of disintegration into coherent and great works.

Let us direct our attention, for example, to Gustav Mahler. He is a composer of whose significance we have become fully aware only today. I agree completely with Luigi Rognoni, who stated in his *Viennese School of Music*:

> Expressionism and Dodecaphony that, from the new point of view, Gustav Mahler appears before us as the precursor of the most complex and varied achievements of the contemporary musical sensibility, and also as a prophet of the human tragedy characteristic of our epoch....[61]

In the Hapsburg metropolis, this great provincial revealed himself as a genius of synthesis. Although the Viennese writer and critic Hermann Bahr called the generation to which they both belonged the "fragmentary" generation ("*Fragmentarisch geblieben...so sieht sich meine Generation*"),[62] Mahler contended with the temptation of the integral work. Like Beethoven, Haydn and Bruckner, he reached for the form of the symphony and made it into a tool for integrating the world. Mahler had no fear of eclecticism. As he said,

> For me, the symphony means constructing a world using all available technical means.[63]

It now remains for musicologists to determine the way in which that method, employed for the maximum "broadening" [*Steigerung*] of the image and the feeling of internal and external reality, led the post–Romantic musical language, with the final push by Schoenberg, to a decisive crash and contributed to the "demise of the tonal system".

The most important thing for me at the moment is the recognition that Mahler's cycle of nine symphonics constitutes the most absorbing and, at the same time, in terms of their musical language, the most autonomous record of the world and mankind in a dramatic moment of crisis—a record in which we can find ourselves. Mahler is our contemporary. We could join Kandinsky in saying,

> this is our harmony—the contention of tones, the lost equilibrium, the collapsing principles, the unexpected striking of the drum, the great questions, the apparently purposeless desires, the apparently sundered aspirations and nostalgia, the broken links and bonds, multiplicity reduced to unity, opposition and contradiction."[64]

In his latest novel, *Immortality*, Milan Kundera called Mahler's symphonies "cathedrals of uselessness."[65] Setting aside this stipulation of utility, so astounding in a writer like Kundera, I find myself unable to see a better example to which we could turn at the present crossroads than Mahler.

In full awareness of the difficulty of the task, I have turned to the form of the symphony in order to absorb and process the experience of our century. When I asked repeatedly about the sense and possibility of constructing an ark, I was thinking of the symphony—that musical ark which would make it possible to convey to coming generations what is best in our twentieth–century tradition of the composing of sounds.

I have often pondered the lack of a universal musical idiom in our century. The musical "common language" present in earlier ages was made possible by the fact that musicians and their audiences accepted certain fixed points of reference. Composers of the twentieth century, while revolutionizing the existing foundations of music, found themselves at a certain moment in a void. The postulate of radical individualism and experimentation has brought about the shattering of all enduring points of sustenance.

It is hardly surprising that the form of the symphony should come to life just now, in the twilight of the epoch. The symphony is a capacious form. One must have something to fill it with. Having reached the limit of its potential, the twentieth century still needs a recapitulation.

My First Symphony was written in 1973, when I was forty. That is a time when one crosses a shadow line. I was then attempting to make a reckoning of my two decades' worth of musical experience—a time of radical, avant–garde seeking. It was the summa of what I could say as an avant–garde artist. The four symmetrical parts *Archē I, Dynamis I, Dynamis II,* and *Archē II* attested to a desire to rebuild the world from scratch. The great destruction, in line with avant–garde logic, simultaneously marked the desire for a new cosmogony.

The Second Symphony ("Christmas Eve"), finished seven years later, referred fully to the late–nineteenth–century symphonic tradition—Wagner, Bruckner, Mahler, Sibelius and Shostakovich—filtered through the sensibility and means of expression of a composer who had experienced the avant–garde. The earlier intention of re–founding the world gives way to the need for internalization and for describing the drama of existence. I could say, in Mahler's words, that my music refers to "the whole man," to the "feeling, thinking, breathing, suffering man."[66]

As the years went by and I passed over successive thresholds, the retrospective imperative grew increasingly strong. I finished my Third Symphony last year, although my Fourth and Fifth Symphonies come before it, chronologically. After its Munich world premiere, a critic discerned in my Third Symphony the outlines of a "creative synthesis." Was that supposed to mean that I was approaching the goal I had set for myself? I would like the answer to that question to be found in my projected Sixth, Eighth and Ninth Symphonies.

Anyone who feels inclined to call my symphonies further instances of "cathedrals of uselessness" should know that I freed myself a long time ago of the temptation of saving the world. I am far more concerned with saving what is most important for me in the artistic and human dimension.

In his visionary poem "The Unfinished Symphony," Oskar Miłosz addresses *Storge*—"his earthly sister" and "sinful love from the other world"—in the belief that she will help him to describe a circle and achieve the mythical time "of the beautiful half–obscured days of childhood summer." *Storge* comes to his aid, but not completely:

> Yet under the burden of mountains of twilights
> I felt that Love, like an internal sun,
> Rose above the lands of memory,
> and that I was flying,
> Far, far away—as in my dream journeys.
> (. . .)

And I thought of what I was to see again,
for there
Lay beautiful archipelagoes and islands
With misty interiors, pure, which had vanished
With the coral grave of my youth.[67]

Must such a symphony remain unfinished?

NOTES

1. From an address delivered in 1868 and quoted by Stanisław Tarnowski in *Julian Klaczko*, Vol. 2 (Kraków, 1909), p. 69.

2. Thomas Mann, *Joseph und seine Brüder* [Joseph and His Brother], Vol. III (*Joseph, der Ernährer*) (Stockholm: Berman–Fischer Verlag, 1948), p. 170.

3. Ranier Maria Rilke, *Wiersze* (Wrocław–Warszawa–Kraków–Gdańsk, 1976), p. 126.

4. Czesław Miłosz, *Nieobjęta ziemia* [The Unknown Land] (Kraków: Wydawnictwo Literackie, 1988), p. 39.

5. Italo Calvino, *Dokładność* [exactness], trans. Justyna Łukaszewicz, *Odra* nr. 3, 1994, p. 27.

6. *Ibid.*

7. L'Abbé [Jacques] De Lille, *Les Jardins, ou l'art d'embellir les paysages. Poème* (Paris: Chez Lacombe, 1782), p. 10.

8. Gustav René Hocke, *Die Welt als Labyrinth. Manier und Manie in der europäischen Kunst. Von 1520 bis* 1650 *und in der Gegenwart* (Hamburg: Rowohlt, 1983), p. 101.

9. Jerzy Pawlas, "Od malarstwa informel do teatru śmierci. Rozmowa z Tadeuszem Kantorem," [From informal painting to the Theatre of Death: an interview with Tadeusz Kantor], *Tygodnik Kulturalny* nr. 5, (1977), p. 5.

10. Czesław Miłosz, "W Szetejniach" [in Szetejny], *Na brzegu rzeki* [Facing the River; New Poems] (Kraków: Wydawnictwo Znak, 1994), p. 77

11. Amos Oz, "Gangster w noc długich noży albo sen" [The ganster in the night of long knives, or a dream] *Ex Libris* nr 60 (1994), p. 2.

12. [Wassily] Kandinsky, *Über das Gestige in der Kunst, inbesondere in der Malerei* (München: R. Pipper & Co. Verlag, 1912), p. 11.

13. Dwight McDonald, "Teoria kultury masowej" [Theory of mass culture] In: *Kultura masowa* [Mass culture], ed. Czesław Miłosz (Paris: Bibiloteka Kultury, 1959), p. 15.

14. William A. Henry III, *In Defense of Elitism* (New York, 1994), p. 14.

15. Józef Bocheński, *Sto zabobonów. Króti filozoficzny słownik zabobonów* (Kraków: Philed, 1992), p. 44

16. *Ibid.*

17. [Wassily] Kandinsky, *op. cit.*, p. 14.

18. The term was coined by the French critic Paul Virilio; see: Marek Bieńbczyk, "Homo pyknolepticus", *Nova Res Publica* 3 (1995), p. 6–10.

19. Zbigniew Herbert, "Babylon," trans. John and Bogdana Carpenter, In: *Raport z oblężonego Miasta i inne wiersze*

[Report from the Besieged City] (Wrocław: Wydawnictwo Dolnośląskie, 1993), p. 49

20. Mieczysław Porębski, "Tradycje i awangardy" [Tradition and avant–garde], In: *Sztuka a informacja* (Kraków: Wydawnictwo Literackie, 1986), p. 171.

21. Czesław Miłosz, *Świadecwo poezji. Sześć wykładów o dotkliwościach naszego wieku* [The testimony of poetry. Six essays on the sore points of our century] (Paris: Institut Literacki, 1983), p. 9.

22. Ludwika Malewska–Mostowicz, *Posłanie ze świata idealnego. Ostatnia rozmowa z Witoldem Lutosławskim,* Rzeczpospolita nr 6 (February 12–13, 1994), p. 11.

23. Quoted by Stanisław Brzozowski, *Legenda Młodej Polski. Studya o strukturze duszy kulturalnej* (Lwów, 1910), reprinted by Wydawnictwo Literacki, Kraków–Wrocław, 1983, p. 123.

24. Oswald Spengler, *Der Untergang des Abendlandes* (Munich, 1923), p. 139. See also Marian Zdziechowski, *Jak upadają cywilizacje* In: *W obliczu końca* (Vilnius, 1938), p. 145.

25. The concept was originated by Louis Pauwels, the founder of the review "Question de. . . ." See also Mircea Eliade, Homo faber 'et' Homo religiosus, In: *Briser le toit de la maison. La créativité et ses symboles* (Paris: Gallimard, 1990), p. 339.

26. See, for example, Danuta Dowjat, *Smutek konca wieku. Wystawa w Tate Gallery*, "Gazeta Wyborcza" (August 29, 1995), p. 10 [review of the exhibition *Rites of Passage: Art for the End of the Century*].

27. Tadeusz Kantor, *XII Lekcja Mediolańska. Przed końicem XX wieku* [Twelfth Milano Lesson. Before the End of the Twentieth Century] In: *Lekcje mediolańskie*, Cricoteka I Biuro Kongresowe Urzędu Miasta Krakowa (Kraków, 1991), p. 98.

28. *Ibid.*

29. Guido Ceronetti, *Drzewa bez Bogów* [The tree without gods], ed. Stanisław Kasprzysiak, (Kraków: Oficyna Literacka, 1995), p. 25.

30. Mircea Eliade, *Briser le toit de la maison*, *op. cit.*, p. 338. [see note 25]

31. Guillaume Apollinaire, "Duch nowych czasów i poeci" [The spirit of the new times and the poets), In: *Wybor pism* [Selected writings], ed. Maciej Żurowski (Warszawa: PIW, 1980), p. 742.

32. Mircea Eliade, *Aspects du mythe* (Paris: Gallimard, 1963), p. 100.

33. *Księga Psalmów*, tłumaczył z hebrajskiego Czesław Miłosz [Book of Psalms, Thalmutic and Hebrew] (Paris: Éditions du Dialogue, 1982), p. 55.

34. Quoted in Ernst Robert Curtius, *Europäischer Literatur und Lateinisches Mittelalter* (Bern, 1948), n.p.

35. Oskar Miłosz, *Storge*, ed. Czesław Miłosz (Kraków: Wydawnictwo Znak, 1993), p. 35

36. *Ibid*, pp. 67–68.

37. *Ibid*, p. 68.

38. Czesław Miłosz, "Introduction in Oskar Miłosz, In: *Storge*..., p. 13.

39. Ernst Bloch, *Abschied von der Utopie?* [Farewell to Utopia?] "Vorträge," ed. Hanna Gekle (Frankfurt/Main: Suhrkamp, 1980), p. 79.

40. *Conflits. Fin de siècle*, "Le Monde Diplomatique" (February 29, 1996)

41. Paul Valéry, *Variété* (Paris, 1924), pp. 39–40.

42. Quoted in Jan Balbierz, *Georg Steiner, krytyk epoki poslowia*, "Teksty Drugie" nr 2/3 (1996), p. 216.

43. *Ibid.*, p. 219.

44. Czesław Miłosz, "Przedmowa" [Introduction] Oskar Miłosz, *Storge* ..., p. 9.

45. Hartmut Böhme, *Teologia teleobecności*, trans. Aleksandra Ubertowska, "Magazyn Sztuki" nr 2 (1966), p. 222.

46. Zbigniew Herbert, "O Troi" [On Troy], In: *Struna światła* [String of light] (Wrocław: Wydawnictwo Dolnośląskie, 1994), p. 27.

47. *Ibid*, pp. 28–29.

48. Josif Brodsky, *Siedząc w cieniu* [Sitting in the shade], In: *Fin de siècle*, ed. Katarzyna Krzyżewska (Kraków: Oficyna Literacka, 1966), p. 22.

49. Anna M. Konormicka, *Słownik zwrotów I aluzji biblijnych* (Łódź: Archidiecezjalne Wydawnictwo Łódżkie, 1994), p. 50.

50. *Sermones R. P. Fratis Heronymi Savonarolea in Adventu Domini super Archam Noe* (Venice, 1536).

51. Gustaw Herling–Grudziński, *Don Ildebrando*, "Rzeczpospolita" nr 162 (July 13–14, 1996), p. 14.

52. Quoted in Valentine Marcadé, *Le renouveau de l'art pictural russe* (1863–1914) (Lausanne: L'Age d'Homme, 1971), p. 134

53. *Das bunte Leben. Wassily Kandinsky im Lenbachhaus.* Stadtische Galerie im Lenbachaus, München, 29 XI 1995 – 10 III 1996.

54. Wassily Kandinsky, "Die Bilder," In: *Arnold Schoenberg in höchster Verehrungn* (München, 1912), quoted by Luigi Rognoni, *Wiedeńska szkoła muzyczna. Ekspresjonizm i dodekafonia* (Kraków: PWM, 1978), p. 483.

55. Quoted by Johannes Eichner, *Wassily Kandinsky und Gabriele Münter* (Munich, 1957), p. 115.

56. *Sermones R. P. Fratris Hieronymi Savonarolae...*, p. 6.

57. Mircea Eliade, *Traktat o historii religii* [Treatise on the history of religion] (Warszawa: Książka i Wiedza, 1966), p. 200.

58. Igor Stravinsky, *Poetyka muzyczna* [The Poetics of Music], ed. Stefan Jarociński, *Res Facta* 4 (1970), p. 200.

59. Italo Calvino, *Wykłady amerykańskie* [American lectures] ed. Anna Wasilewska (Gdańsk–Warszawa: Oficyna Wydawnicza Volumen, 1996).

60. Quoted in *Postmodernism. ICA Documents*, ed. Lisa Appignanesi (London: Free Association Books, 1989), p. 112.

61. Luigi Rognoni, *Wiedelska Szkoła* [The Viennese School], *op. cit.*, p. 19.

62. Quoted by Pierre–Yves Petillon, *Hoffmanstahl ou le règne du silence. Fragments à propos de Lord Chandos*, "Critique" nr 339–340 (Special issue, *Vienne, dēbut dun siècle*, 1975), p. 900.

63. Bohdan Pociej, *Mahler* (Kraków: PWM, 1992), p. 179.

64. [Wassily] Kandinsky, *Über das Geistige in der Kunst, inbesondere in der Maleiei* (München: R. Pipper and Co. Verlag, 1912), p. 91–92.

65. Milan Kundera, *Nieśmiertelność*, [Immortality], ed. Marek Bieńczyk (Warszawa: PWI, 1996), p. 378.

66. From a 1906 letter to Bruno Walter in which Mahler announces the completion of his Sixth Symphony. Quoted in Ulrich Schreiber, *Gustav Mahler: une musique des contradictions sociales*, "Critique" nr 339–340 (1975), p. 934.

67. Oskar Miłosz, "Nie dokończona symfonia" [The unfinished symphony], In: *Storge...*, p. 30.

KRZYSZTOF PENDERECKI'S 'LABYRINTH OF TIME': CONVERSATIONS AT THE END OF THE MILLENNIUM

An interview given to Ray Robinson
at the Plaza Hotel, New York City on October 26, 1997

Krzysztof, when your extensive career as a composer is viewed at the end of this millennium, there is a tendency to identify a number of style periods or compositional phases in your music. Is this a correct analysis? Or would you describe the evolution of your compositional style in other terms?

I now see only one stream of development in my music from the beginning until now. Starting with the Psalms of David, which was my first step as a composer, and where I discovered the elements of my own musical language for the first time, until the most recent two pieces [*Seven Gates of Jerusalem* and *Hymn to the Holy Daniel*]. Even in the melodic approach and the structure of, for example,

Seven Gates, you will find elements in the Psalms I wrote as a student in 1958. Of course there are periods where I have been fascinated by the avant–garde or fascinated by late–romantic music. As a result there are some pieces that are very close to the avant–garde and romantic movements. Elements of romantic music were present in my works during the 1980s. But this is only for a short period. Then I went away from what I did, and I looked for something else. For example, after the very avant–garde pieces like *String Quartet No. 1* and *Fluorescences*, in the same year (1962) I wrote *Stabat mater*, which is a totally different piece. Then after the very romantic *Violin Concerto No. 1* (1976) and the *Symphony No. 2* (1980), a few years later I wrote *The Black Mask* (1986) which is an anti–romantic piece. Following a very serious piece like the *Polish Requiem* (1980–84), I wrote an opera buffa, *Ubu Rex* (1991). But this is the same music really.

This pattern is present in all my works. After a period of search, as in *Stabat mater*, I simplified my musical language. Next I turned to tradition, the Netherlands school and to polyphony and counterpoint. Since the *Awakening of Jacob* (1974), I have sought a synthesis between the avant–garde style of my earlier works and a more expressive [romantic] musical language. This synthesis was achieved in the opera *The Black Mask*. I believe that the same musical elements are present in my works from the 1950's until now.

Did this discovery of synthesis in your musical language take place quickly or did its evolution occur over a long period of time?

This change of style, or course, did not happen from one day to the next. There was a long period of development that began in the 1970's, with pieces like *Awakening of Jacob*, in which I started to change my style, through works like *Te Deum* and the *Symphony No. 2*, which are what you might call romantic. But then I turned away from this style. The opera *The Black Mask* was really the piece that fully revealed this style change; this is the work in which I achieved this synthesis. It is the style that I am writing in until now.

Then you would say that this final synthesis begins in the 1970s and reaches its fulfillment in 1986 with the opera *The Black Mask*, even though there are elements of this style evident throughout this period.

Yes, this work was the turning point in my musical thinking. I have always talked about the need to renew the musical language in contemporary music, especially in the 1960's and 1970's. Every composer tried to do something different. There was not the unity in the style which is found in the 19th century. Every composer wrote almost in the same style in this period.

You are speaking of the avant–garde composers in the 1950's and 1960's?

Yes.

Has your extensive conducting career played a role in achieving this synthesis?

Yes, I think so. I remember performing the pieces which I composed in the 1960's—like the *St. Luke Passion*—and the conductor would have thirteen rehearsals to prepare this work. Now you never get more than four. This was my first realization that these early works required so much rehearsal time, so much explanation; this doesn't work now. Since I changed the orchestral parts, I am preparing this piece in a three hour rehearsal. Also the experience with orchestra has influenced my writing for orchestra. I am now writing more for instruments, not the abstract kind of music that is associated with my style in the 1960's.

Let me get this straight. Are you saying that your work with the major symphony orchestras of the world led you to conclude that a less experimental style would produce more effective results.

This happened not only to me but to almost all my colleagues. The kind of style in which we composed in the 1950's and 1960's has almost disappeared. First, it's not needed, and, of course, it's impossible to repeat. We live in another time now. Everything was done in the 1960's to create an avant–garde style, to develop a new musical language, to come up with new techniques for instruments, and to introduce new instruments in the orchestra. Of course, electronic music, which was a very important factor at that time, was also an influence on the style. But now at the end of our century we do not need to do this anymore. The 1960's represent a very important historic movement, but we cannot repeat that style today.

What about the world–wide musical audience that hears your music? Has your perception of their

changing needs, tastes, and desires been a factor in this synthesis?

Maybe, but not that I would decide to change my style to please the audience. Of course, you know that the pieces I wrote in the 1960's were also very successful. . . . No, I do not think that the audience has influenced this synthesis.

You have often reflected on the absence of a universal musical idiom in our century. In the Viennese Classical period, for example, there was a so–called "common practice" among composers. Is the synthesis you have achieved in your more recent works in any sense an attempt to create such a universal musical idiom?

Yes, I have been talking about this since the 1960's. The best example was the *St. Luke Passion*; it was my first attempt to find a musical language that was not only modern but which also employed some elements from the past. I was trying to find a co–existence between the very avant–garde style of my experimental works and the past. I made the first step in *Stabat mater*, before the *Passion*. This is where I discovered the polyphonic style that allowed me later to write the *St. Luke Passion* and other pieces. But this was the result of studying 16th century counterpoint. It was a different kind of counterpoint, of course, but the idea was to try to incorporate both elements. In *Stabat mater* you have the polyphonic style of many voices—twelve different lines, twelve voices—but you also have the cluster, which was an avant–garde technique of the 1960's. Here, in this work, we find both elements.

Then you took this style to an extreme in the pieces of the early 1970's, works like *Magnificat* and *Ecloga VIII* which contained very complicated polyphony.

Stabat mater, of course, was the beginning; the *St. Luke Passion* was much more complicated because I used instruments with voices: it contained techniques which are found in my instrumental pieces of the early 1960's. But *Magnificat* is also the last piece where I used a very complicated polyphonic technique; here you find 48 different voices. This makes the piece almost impossible to perform. You need fifty rehearsals to prepare this piece.

What are some of the definable characteristics of this so–called "universal musical language" about which you have been speaking? Is this something you can define and discuss?

The main idea was to find a musical language which was appropriate, not only for me and my music, but for our time. The kind of orchestration that I used in the 1960's was so individual that it could only be used for my music. It was not adaptable to the works of other composers. But the music that I am writing now, which also contains elements from the past, though transformed to the idiom of our time, is something that has a more universal application. For example, the kind of orchestration that is closer to a composer like Bruckner: the density of sound caused by doubling parts in the orchestra. This universal style has elements from the late–nineteenth century, a period I adore very much. But there are also elements from the avant–garde.

When I listen to the Penderecki works which have been written in the last two decades, I think of another kind of "synthesis": one which reflects a coming together of the various musical styles of this century. When one thinks of the Baroque period in music history–the musical expression of the years 1600 to 1750–there is a tendency to credit Bach and Handel with a kind of summary statement of that period. Have you made a conscious effort in your later works (1975–2000) to codify any of the musical innovations in this millennium?

Yes, I think so; I am trying. I do not know whether I will succeed or what will happen to my music in 50 years. Look what happened to music in the last years of the previous century. Mahler was taking everything from the whole century, writing his own music, but using the technique from other composers and developing it . What I am doing is writing my music. Of course there are some elements from other composers: Shostakovich. Bartok, Stravinsky, etc.

So you have made a concerted effort to bring together in your music some of the musical innovations of our century?

Yes

Your musical language today is fascinating. It sounds new, yet its roots are in the oldest traditions of musical composition.

Well for me it's new because it's a new experience for me. It's something which maybe goes back a little in time, but it goes back in order to go forward. It's a problem with which not only I, but a lot of composers have had to deal. With all the complications of the new discoveries in music, we had to stop our lives and to think about history, to think about tradition, which is very important. I have always talked about the importance of tradition. Without tradition, I couldn't write the St.Luke Passion or the other large pieces which have played such an important role in my career.

Why is tradition such an important influence in your music?

I think tradition is more important to me now because I am older. I would like to continue the music that was cast at the beginning of the century: the tradition of writing symphonies. Sibelius, Bruckner, Shostakovich and Prokofiev were the last composers of my era writing the big forms. Then the tradition disappeared; no one was interested in picking up and continuing these big forms. This continuation is something very inportrant to me, and all I'm doing is trying to carry on a tradition.

I would like to turn for a moment to a discussion of your earlier musical language, a topic that might be of interest to our readers in light of the previous discussion. Who were some of your important musical influences, composers who were prominent at the beginning of this millennium?

Well, in the beginning, while still a student, I discovered composers for myself: first Bartók and Stravinsky (for he was a very strong influence on all Polish music at that time), and then, in 1957, I heard the music of Schoenberg and Webern for the first time.

What were some of those pieces? For example, which work of Webern marked your introduction to his music?

The String Quartet.

And the first composition by Schoenberg? Was it early or late Schoenberg?

It was the later Schoenberg. *A Survivor from Warsaw* was, I think, the first piece I heard. Then his chamber music, his early chamber music, and the modern Psalm ...

... the first Psalm, Op. 50c?

Yes! This music influenced me very much. I started to write serial music as a result of hearing and studying these pieces. I wrote *Emanations* and *Threnody* then, especially the middle part of *Threnody*.

So you were intentionally composing serial music in this early period?

Oh, yes, sure. I did use some serial techniques. For example, I used twelve–tone writing in the *Psalms of David* and the *St. Luke Passion*, but not as strictly as in my instrumental music. For example, the middle section of

Threnody is very strictly written. But I don't use these techniques any more.

I have always been intrigued with your linear (or "melodic") style. It has been more or less consistent throughout your career. Except for examples like the second movement ("Psalm 30") of your *Psalms of David* and the dense middle section of *Threnody*, you have not composed strict "serial" music and you are not known as a "serial" composer. Yet the linear events in all phases and periods of your writing do show the influence of serialism. How do you explain this phenomenon in your music?

This was the result of my early fascination with this style. I discovered serialism very late because of the place where I used to live in Poland. We didn't have scores, we did not have the possibility of hearing this music. I was already a practicing composer at the time when I started to be interested in this music. It fascinated me then and has continued to influence my style until now. I am not writing serial works, of course, but the influence of this period of 20th century music is present in my work.

What about your early musical influences in Poland?

I was trained very traditionally in school. I studied harmony, counterpoint, etc. My professor [Artur Malawski] was against twelve–tone technique so I never wrote any serial music for him. Also Poland was closed to the West until 1956, you know, and new music was not allowed to be played. We did not have the possibility of travelling–it wasn't allowed. We didn't even have scores! Luigi Nono came to visit Poland for the first time in 1957. He brought some scores with him, and he gave me a few. I remember receiving the *Five Pieces for Orchestra* by Webern. I was already writing my own music at that time. He also gave me some of his music. I think they were works like *Il Canto di Spezzo*, *Varianti* for violin and orchestra, *Cori di de Doni*, a piece for chorus, then *Improvisation sur Mallarmé* by Boulez. All this was very new for me, and I tried to incorporate some of these techniques in my music in a very short time. This was in 1958, until the middle of 1959. And then I decided to go my own way.

With a primarily "traditional" background as a student, what caused you to develop the experimental musical language that we find in your works during the years 1958 to 1962, works like *Emanations*, *Threnody*, *Polymorphia*, *Fluorescences*, etc.

Well, first of all, I was a string player. I was at the time still playing and working in the Warsaw Experimental Electronic Music Studio, experimenting with the violin and electronic instruments. As I stated earlier in this interview I wanted to develop a new musical language. But It was not my intention to destroy everything that had written before me. I only wanted to write my own music, so I was experimenting with new sounds; I think the electronic studio helped me at that time in experimenting with all those clusters that you find in the works which you listed above.

Were the sounds that resulted from these experiments something that you heard in the electronic

studio and were trying to duplicate with "real" instruments?

No, I would say it was more the result of experimenting with the instrument itself; it was the search for new sounds with stringed instruments. But, of course, I think that pure electronic music also influenced me at that time.

What caused you to continue this search for new musical sonorities even after you had stopped your work in the Experimental Electronic Studio?

Well, except for the early period, when the instruments then available did not satisfy me, I always treated them as a musical contingency. The purpose was to find sounds that would correspond to my musical ideas or an instrument which would create the desired atmosphere...not necessarily to discover a new instrument.

I recently read a quotation where you stated: "Art is in essence constructive. Revolution entails a disturbance. ..." When you were carrying on these experiments and developing this experimental musical language did you believe that "revolution" was necessary?

Absolutely! And until now I believe in the revolution. I am pretty sure that in the next century, perhaps in the beginning or maybe later, there will emerge a group of younger musician–composers who will find something new. I do not know what, because we cannot predict what will take place in the future. We are now busy trying to find a synthesis, not only I but other composers are engaged in this search. This is the turn of the century and this search is very typical for composers at this time.

At what point in your career did you decide that revolution was not the way for Penderecki?

I was a revolutionary in my early years, very much believing in this, but then step by step I discovered very simply that this was not the only way to express what I wanted to say as a composer. This kind of music was not enough, it was and is very much limited.

Are you saying that at a certain point in your career your musical instincts led you to the conclusion that the internationally respected avant–garde movement was a dead end. That after *Fluorescences*, the most experimental of your instrumental works, and *Magnificat*, which played a similar role in your vocal writing, there was no place to go.

Absolutely, maybe only to electronic music.

In one of your recent lectures you quoted a famous statement by Igor Stravinsky: "I have been made a revolutionary against my will!" How is this possible when you were a leader rather than a follower in the avant–garde movement of your time?

But this was a very short time. I was very much a revolutionary in the late–1950s...until *Stabat mater* [1962]. And then I was trying to find a way out of this movement. I was writing music against all my colleagues, the avant–garde composers of the time. Of course, I was very much criticized for that. But this was really a very short period of my career.

As someone who has observed your work over a long period of time, I believe that a significant and perceptible change in the nature of your musical language can be identified in works composed after the political changes in 1989. The Polish musicologist Regina Chłopicka has perceived this change as "a shift of gravity towards the circle of light, goodness and pure beauty." This change can be analyzed musically as a considerable reduction in musical means (for example, the chamber works and the short pieces for unaccompanied chorus), as a balance of formal proportions, an opera buffa, and what seems to be a more personal musical language. Do you believe that the events of 1989 in Poland had any impact on your career as a composer?

No I don't think so. It was a big political change, and it also influenced me very much. For example, today I would not write music that was involved in a political movement like, for example, the [Polish] *Requiem* and other pieces. Because of the situation in Poland before 1989 I wouldn't write an opera buffa like *Ubu Rex.* I actually started to write the opera *Ubu Rex* in the early 1980s, but it was impossible to continue it under martial law. So instead of an opera buffa, I wrote the *Requiem.* Then after the political change, *Ubu Rex.*

Throughout your career—from Strophes (1959) to Ubu Rex (1990)—many of your works have been

associated with humanistic and symbolic ideas in the form of social, national and universal themes. Works like *Threnody for the Victims of Hiroshima*, *The Devils of Loudun*, *Te Deum* and the *Polish Requiem* are examples of this tendency in your music. While I realize that you no longer feel that you can change the world through your music, as you once did, is not the plight of your fellow man still of concern to you as a composer?

This was not really political music that I was writing, but it was music that was appropriate to the time during which we were living in Poland. Now I think I've changed my mind about this. My music today is not so involved in anything; it is not so dense and expressive as it used to be in those years. I think with age I have found distance from the time in which I am living. This is why I was able to write the buffa piece. But you can find this element in the other works as well.

Is there a chance that in the future you might encounter another repressive political situation, for example, like the current situation in Bosnia, or one where there is a universal idea involved, and compose a work to highlight such an injustice?

No. I was very idealistic as a young man. I was raised in the post–World War II time. It was very difficult for us in Poland because for us the war really ended in 1989, not in 1945. Now I would never write a piece which contained a political message. I am free from that now.

What are your thoughts of the function of the composer as we come to the end of this millennium? Have they changed over the years?

Of course they have changed since the 1950s because at that time I was living in a special place in Eastern Europe and I was very much concerned with what was going on. We were always rebelling against the government. Even my early music—the avant–garde music—was a kind of protest against the "official" kind of music which they [the government officials] asked us to write. The official music, of course, was the music of "social realism". They tried to force us to write in this style (almost nobody in Poland wrote this kind of music), but most of the composers from Russia, Bulgaria, Czechoslavia did compose this type of music. We were free from that because Russia did not try to "crush" us. Now living in a free society and under a democratic system I do not feel a need anymore to write music of protest.

If a student asked you to define the function of the composer at the end of the millennium, what would you say?

To entertain. The purpose of art is to entertain. Of course, you can write a serious piece to entertain, but you can also entertain with an opera buffa. I do not think there is any difference in regard to the function of the composer between the eighteenth, nineteenth and the end of the twentieth century.

On the surface, at least, it seems that you have reached a point in your career where composing

comes very easy. Even with the time limitations caused by your busy conducting schedule, your gardens at your country home in Lusławice, and your family and professional responsibilities, you are able to turn out new works on a regular basis: symphonies, large choral works, concertos, etc. Is it as easy as it seems?

No, it is not true! Knowing that I am always travelling, you do not know when I am writing. First of all, I am writing every day. I am working in a concentrated environment sometimes only a half an hour during a day. I am always writing new pieces. So it is not that the music just flows from me.

So you are working as hard as ever to produce these new compositions.

Even more! And I am preparing a piece for a very long time. For example, the *Hymn to the Holy Daniel* (premiered October 1997 in Moscow) is only a fifteen minute piece, yet it took me four months to finish it. So I am not a person to which writing comes easily. Given my time limitations, I have found that it is now more difficult than ever before for me to write music.

At the end this millennium, when the musical language of many of your avant–garde contemporaries has lost its appeal to the listener, you are more popular than ever. Do you feel that you are reaching your audience today?

Yes, I think so, but not because I try to reach them. I have changed by style in the last few years but I am still writing big form works for large orchestra. Even my early pieces, like *Threnody*, have a large orchestra. I think I'm writing for me, to please myself, but if others like my music, I'm pleased too.

Now you have an extensive career as a conductor as well as that of a composer. How do you balance these two responsibilities and keep composing while travelling around the world conducting? Is it difficult to have a dual career?

Yes, it is a great problem for me because I am conducting too much–more than 60 concerts a year–and taking too many performances that maybe I shouldn't take. But the main reason why I'm doing it is because I am presenting my music to the audience; and the audience, if the composer is conducting, thinks that maybe this is the correct way to hear it. It's not always so, and the composer is often in jeopardy because his perception is very limited. It is only my way of doing it, and there could be other ways to do the same piece differently, and also, well!

We are rapidly approaching the end of the millennium. How would you like your contribution to the 20th century to be remembered by those who are charged with the task of writing the history of this millennium?

First of all, I am trying to be sincere in what I am doing. As you know I am not a composer who is very much influenced by what is happening in the musical world now. I have always been going alone; I have gone my own way throughout my career. Even my avant–garde period was different from others. It was going against my colleagues from Darmstadt and Donaueschingen.

Second, I would like to be remembered as a composer who has a personal style, even one that is influenced by the entire century. This is really what I wanted. Not to write very original music only which would not give me an opportunity to develop what I wanted to say. I want to say different things and that is why my music is different. Each two or three years I am adding something which is new; I am always searching for something which is new. I would never write according to a formula. If you look at my symphonies, you will discover that each is different.

What will be your final musical work for this millennium? Is there one form, one text, one idea that will serve as a summary statement of your musical thinking for the 20th century?

I am planning to write a Christmas Oratorio for the year 2000, to commemorate two thousand years of Christianity. Since I am Christian and compose as a Christian, I must write a major religious work. I am considered a composer of religious music. While this is not entirely true, since I have written other types of music, I have composed many religious works. Looking at other composers of our time, there is only one–Olivier Messiaen–who has written as much music on sacred texts. This is my task. After that I will probably not write any other oratorios. I have composed so many large choral works. I am not sure that I will be able to find ideas for another work of this type

But you will continue to compose instrumental works?

Yes. I want to continue writing symphonies. I consider my symphonic music to be very important. The Sympnoy No. 6 will be ready in two years. I am one of the few living composers who is still interested in the big symphonic form which, of course, has its roots in the music of the eighteenth and nineteenth centuries. In my symphonic works you can find elements of Beethoven and Bruckner through Prokofiev and Shostakovich and, of course, Sibelius.

You have recently signed a commissioning agreement with the Munich Philharmonic. How many symphonies will you compose for them?

My agreement with Munich calls for three additional symphonies. The *Seven Gates of Jerusalem*, composed for the 3000th anniversary of Jerusalem, is Symphony No. 7. I will write six, eight and nine for the Munich Philharmonic.

Will No. 9 be a "choral" symphony?

I am not sure. *Seven Gates of Jerusalem* is a choral symphony [Symphony No. 7] that is already completed.

Is No. 6 scheduled for 1999?

Yes, I have sketches. This will be a very long, very large work. I am not sure I will finish it before the year 2000.

Will you really stop at 9?

Yes, I think so. There is something symbolic about this?

The symbolism of a ninth symphony is indeed an appropriate place to conclude this interview. I trust that your five lectures and this fascinating interview will give your English–speaking readers new insights into the way you have approached your art in your own personal "Labyrinth of Time". Thank you so much for sharing these very personal thoughts with us.

PENDERECKI'S TEXTS

TEXTS COMPILED BY KRZYSZTOF PENDERECKI

DIES IRAE (1967)

Dies irae was written in 1967 in memory of all those who died at Auschwitz. It is a powerful and highly dramatic musical invocation of the horror, pain and inhuman depravity that the Nazi's inflicted on their victims. It was performed in Auschwitz on April 16, 1967, on the occasion of the unveiling of the International Monument to the Victims of Fascism at Auschwitz–Birkenau.

The text setting is unusual in one respect: it does not employ the traditional Requiem sequence for the dead, nor does it quote the well–known chant theme, but instead consists of various Biblical passages, modern French and Polish poems, and excerpts from the *Furies* of Aeschylus. The work is in three movements.

I. Lamentatio

The sorrows of death compassed me…[Psalm 116]

Bodies of children
From crematories
Will fly
High above history
Bodies of boys,
Bodies of girls
In crowns of thorns
Will flock together.
Bodies of men

From field–graveyards
Will march to conquer,
Will be free. [Broniewski *Ciała* (Bodies)]

The utmost hunger and the limits of strength
Even Christ did not follow such a path of doom
He never knew that racking discord
Between a human soul and an inhuman world.
[Aragon (Auschwitz)]

Bodies from camps
From murdered cities,

Bodies with halters,
Bodies with wounds,
Bodies of doom,
Bodies of wrong
Will come in hosts,
Will never rest. [Broniewski *Ciała* (Bodies)]

In huge crates
Dry hair–tufts billow
Of strangled people,
And a small braid,
A pigtail with a ribbon,
Pulled in a class–room
By naughty boys.
[Różewicz *Warkoczyk* (A Pigtail)]

II. Apocalypsis

Let him that hath understanding count the number of
the beast: for it is the number of a man.
[Revelation 13]

...song of the Furies
binding brain and blighting blood
in its stringless melody.
[Aeschylus *The Eumenides* 331–333]

And I saw a beast rise up out of the sea, having seven
heads and ten horns, and upon his horns ten crowns,
and upon his heads the name of blasphemy.
[Revelation 13]

And the great dragon was cast out, that old serpent,
called the Devil, and Satan, which deceiveth the
whole world: he was cast out into the earth.
[Revelation 12]

Over the beast doomed to the fire
this is the chant, scatter of wits,
frenzy and fear, hurting the heart,
song of the Furies
binding brain and blighting blood
in its stringless melody.
[Aeschylus *The Eumenides* 328–333]

...and all the world wondered after the beast.
And they worshiped the dragon which gave power
unto the beast, and they worshiped the beast,
saying: Who is like unto the beast? who is able to

make war with him? And there was given unto
him a mouth speaking great things and blasphemies;
and power was given unto him to continue forty
and two months.
[Revelation 13]

. . . and the holy city tread they under foot forty
and two months. [Revelations 11]

For the great day of his wrath is come; and
who shall be able to stand? [Revelations 6]

Come then, link we our choral.
Ours to show forth the power
and terror of our music, declare
our rights of office, how we
conspire to steer men's lives.
[Aeschylus *The Emenides* 307–311]

After this I beheld, and, lo, a great multitude, which
no man could number, of all nations, and kindreds,
and people, and tongues. [Revelation 7]

Fear none of those things which thou shalt suffer:
behold, the devil shall cast some of you into prison,
that ye may be tried; and ye shall have tribulations
ten days: be thou faithful unto death, and I will give
thee a crown of life. He that overcometh shall not
be hurt of the second death. [Revelations 2]

Over the beast doomed to the fire
this is the chant, scatter of wits,

frenzy and fear, hurting the heart,
song of the Furies
binding brain and blighting blood
in its stringless melody.
[Aeschylus *The Emenides* 328–333]

. . . as many as would not worship the image of the beast should be killed.
[Revelation 13]

For with a long leap from high
above and dead drop of weight
I bring foot's force crashing down
to cut the legs from under even
the runner, and spill him to ruin.
[Aeschylus *The Emenides* 372–376]

And he was clothed with a vesture dipped in blood.
[Revelation 19]

And I saw the beast, and the kings of the earth, and their armies, gathered together to make war against him that sat on the horse, and against his army. And the beast was taken, and with him the false prophet. . . . These both were cast alive into a lake of fire burning with brimstone. And the remnant were slain with the sword of him that sat upon the horse, which sword proceeded out of his mouth; and all the fowls were filled with their flesh.
[Revelation 19]

III. Apothesis

Death is swallowed up in victory.
[I Corinthians 15]

And I saw a new heaven and a new earth.
[Revelation 21]

Death is swallowed up in victory. O death, where is thy sting? O grave, where is thy victory?
[I Corinthians 15]

The wind rises! . . . . Let us try to live!
[Valéry *Le Cimetière marin*]

COSMOGONY (1970)

Cosmogony was composed on a commission from the United Nations Organization to commemorate the twenty–fifth anniversary of its founding in 1945. It was premiered on October 24, 1970 at the UNO headquarters in New York.

The text is a diverse and wonderfully organized collage of writings and sayings about the cosmos, space and the universe. Quotations from the Bible, Nicolaus di Cusa, Nicolaus Copernicus, T. Lucretius Carus, P. Ovidius Naso, Sophocles, Leonardo di Vince, Giordano Bruno are combined with the words of the astronauts Uri Gagarin and John Glenn, which brings a brilliant touch of historical perspective to man's accomplishments in space. The work's four movements contain one that is orchestral.

I. Origin

The form of the earth is excellent and spherical; its movement circular.
[Nicolaus de Cusa—*De docta ignorantia* 2, 12]

. . . the heavens are held to be immeasurable in comparison to the earth and to have the appearance of infinitive magnitude; but in the estimation of the senses the earth is said to be in relation to the heavens like a point to a solid body and in size like the finite to the infinite.
[Nicolaus Copernicus—*De revolutionibus orbium caelestium* 1, 6]

Space beyond the barriers of this world is boundless, so the reasoning mind seeks to know what may be there and how far the understanding may penetrate and over what

realm the mind set free may fly.
[T. Lucretius Carus—*De rerum natura* 2, 1044–1047]

In the middle of everything however resides the sun. For who could hope to set this burning torch at another better place in this beautiful temple than at that point from where it can illuminate all things at the same time.
[Nicolaus Copernicus—*De revolutionibus arbium caelestium* 1, 6]

. . . and there was light.
[Genesis 1, 3]

We perceive therefore in this system the wondrous symmetry of the world and a certain harmonious connection between movement and the size of the orbits.
[Nicolaus Copernicus—*De revolutionibus arbium caelestium* 1, 10]

For as soon as your reason (Epicurus), begins to declare the nature of the things issuing from Divine Wisdom, the terrors of the soul depart, the walls of this world open, and I see what is being enacted throughout the void.
[T. Lucretius Carus—*De rerum natura* 3, 14–17]

II. The Infinite Universe

Man is needed: the rising sun shines forth, the darkness has vanished.
[P. Ovidius Naso—*Metamorphoses* 2, 144]

The great bird will rise up on its first flight – on the back of this Great Swan, filling the universe with astounding, fill-

ing all books with his name, and eternal fame for his place of birth.
[Leonardo da Vinci —*Sul volo*]

Oh, may Titan (sun) come forth from his Lethean origin, holding back the undulating field (sea), and try to reach the stars – for this I ask. You wandering stars, see how I rise in the same paths, after you have opened the way. Let your movement allow me, as I hurry through the void, to throw apart completely the double doors of sleep.
[Giordano Bruno—*De la causa, principio et uno* 19 (*A i principi de l'universo*)]

The flight is progressing well. I can see the earth, the forests, the clouds, the rivers.
[Uri Gagarin during the first manned space flight]

In the periscope, I can see the brilliant blue horizon coming up behind me; approaching sunrise. Oh, the sun is coming up behind me in the periscope, a brilliant, brilliant red.
[John Glenn during the first United States manned orbital space flight]

The living force of reason has prevailed and has advanced far beyond the flaming walls of the world and has penetrated the whole immeasurable universe with intelligence and spirit. From there he (Epicurus) brings back to us in triumph the answer about what can come about and what cannot; finally, for which reason for each thing only limited possibilities and a deeply rooted boundary–stone exist.

[T. Lucretius Carus—*De rerum natura* 1, 72–77]
There exist many potent powers, but nothing is more powerful than man.
[Sophocles—*Antigone* 332–333]

Thus I stretch my sure wings out in the air; and I fear no barrier of crystal or glass, but cut through the heavens, and I rise into the infinite.
[Giordano Bruno—*De l'infinito universo a mondi*]

"Icarus" he (Daedalus) called, "where are you? In which place should I seek you?"
[P. Ovidius Naso—*Metamorphoses* 8, 232]

I am in a big mass of some very small particles that are brilliantly lit
Up like they're luminescent. I never say anything like it. They round
A little; they're coming by the capsule, and they look like litle stars.
A whole shower of them coming by. . . .
[John Glenn during the first United States manned space flight]

. . . and the immense multitude of the universe was created.
[P. Ovidius Naso—*Metamorphoses* 2, 157]

SEVEN GATES OF JERUSALEM (1996)

Ad maiorem Dei gloriam et euis sanctis civitatis laudem aeternam [Dedicated to the glory of God and His Holy City with eternal praise]

The celebrations surrounding the three thousandth anniversary of the old city of Jerusalem provided the occasion for the commissioning of *Seven Gates of Jerusalem* (Symphony No. 7). The first performance was given on January 7, 1997.

The composer assembled a variety of Old Testament texts for this work, including the Psalms of David and excerpts from writings of the major prophets: the books of Isaiah, Jeremiah, Ezekiel and Daniel. Notwithstanding the fact that the text is taken exclusively from the Old Testament, the composer has stated that the prophetical writings, "especially the passage from Daniel, point to the resurrection and the coming of Christ." There are seven movements.

I.

Great is the Lord and most worthy of praise
in the city of our God, his holy mountain.
[Psalm 48, 1]

Sing to the Lord a new song;
sing to the Lord, all the earth.
Sing to the Lord, praise his name;
proclaim his salvation day after day.
Declare his glory among the nations,
for great is the Lord and most worthy of praise.
[Psalm 96, 1–4]

For this God is our God for ever and ever.
[Psalm 48, 14]

II.
If I forget you, O Jerusalem,
May my right hand forget [its skill].
[Psalm 137, 5]

III.
Out of the depths I cry to you, O Lord.
O Lord, hear my voice;
Let your ears be attentive to my cry for mercy.
If you, O Lord, kept a record of sins,
O Lord, who could stand?
[Psalm 130, 1–3]

IV.
If I forget you, O Jerusalem,
may my right hand forget [its skill].
[Psalm 137, 5]

Open the gates,
that the righteous nation that keeps faith
may enter in.
[Isaiah 26, 2]

Awake, awake, O Zion,
clothe yourself with strength;
put on your garments of splendor;
O Jerusalem, the holy city.
[Isaiah 52, 1]

If I forget you, O Jerusalem,
May my right hand forget [its skill]
[Psalm 137, 5]

V.
Extol the Lord, O Jerusalem
praise you God, O Zion.
For he strengthens the bars of your gates,
and blesses your people within you.
He grants peace to your borders. . . .
Extol the Lord.
Alleluia!
[Psalm 147, 12–14, 20]

VI.
The hand of the Lord was upon me, and he brought me out by the Spirit of the Lord and set me in the middle of a valley; it was full of bones. He led me to and fro among them, and I saw a great many bones on the floor of the valley, bones that were very dry. He asked me, "Son of man, can these bones live?"

I said, "O Sovereign Lord, you alone know." Then he said to me, "Prophesy to these bones and say to them, "Dry bones, hear the word of the Lord! This is what the Sovereign Lord says to these bones: I will make breath enter you, and you will come to life. I will attach tendons to you and make flesh come upon you and cover you with skin; I will put breath in you and you will come to life. Then you will know that I am the Lord.

So I prophesied as I was commanded. And as I was prophesying, there was a noise, a rattling sound, and the bones came together, bone to sound. I looked, and tendon and flesh appeared to them and skin covered them, but there was no breath in them.

Then he said to me, "Prophesy to the breath; prophesy, son of man, and say to it, "This is what the Sovereign Lord says: Come from the four winds, O breath, and breathe into these slain that they may live." So I prophesied as he commanded me, and breath entered them, they came to life and stood upon their feet, a vast army.
[Ezekiel 37, 1–10]

VII.
This is what the Lord says:
See, I am setting before you the way of life and the way of death.
[Jeremiah 21, 8]

And there before me was one like a Son of man,
Coming with the clouds of heaven.
[Daniel 7, 13–14]

From the west, men will fear the name of the Lord,
and from the rising of the sun, they will revere his glory.
For he will come like a pent–up load
that the breath of the Lord drives along.
[Isaiah 59, 19]

Arise shine, Jerusalem,
for your light will come,

and the glory of the Lord rises upon you.
See, darkness covers the earth,
and thick darkness is over the peoples.
But the Lord rises upon you,
and his glory appears over you.
Great is the Lord, and most worthy of praise
In the city of our God.
[Isaiah 60, 1–3]

Your gates will always stand open;
they will never be shut, day or night.
[Isaiah 60, 11]

Sing to the Lord, all the earth,
declare his glory among the nations,
His marvelous deeds among all peoples.
[Psalm 95, 1–3]

Great is the Lord, and most worthy of praise
in the city of our God, his holy mountain.
For this God is our God for ever and ever.
Great is the Lord in the city of our God.
He will be our guide even to the end.
[Psalm 48, 1, 14]

BIOGRAPHICAL SKETCH

KRZYSZTOF PENDERECKI, born in Dębica (Poland) on November 23, 1933, is widely recognized as one of the most important composers of the twentieth century. His extensive and varied work exemplifies the synthesis of the languages of the avant–garde and musical tradition and includes instrumental, choral and operatic compositions. His major works, eleven of which have received their first performances in the United States, include *Threnody to the Victims of Hiroshima* (1960), the *St. Luke Passion* (1966), *Dies irae* (1967), *Utrenya* [Matins] (1970–71), *Cosmogony* (1970); the operas *The Devils of Loudun* (1969), *Paradise Lost* (1978), *The Black Mask* (1986) and *King Ubu* (1991); and the *Polish Requiem* (1980–1993). The composer's instrumental work includes the *Symphony I* (1973), *Symphony II* (1980), *Symphony III* (1988–95), *Symphony IV* (1989) and *Symphony V* (1992); the *Concerto I for Violin* (1976) and *Concerto II for Violin* (1995), *Concerto I for Violoncello* (1972) and *Concerto II for Violoncello* (1983), *Concerto for Viola* (1983), *Concerto for Flute and Chamber Orchestra* (1992). In 1996, Penderecki completed the large work for chorus and orchestra entitled *SevenGates of Jerusalem*, commissioned for the three–thousandth anniversary of the City and premiered on January 9, 1997 under the baton of Lorin Maazel. The oratorio *Credo* was heard for the first time on July 11, 1998, at the Oregon Bach Festival (Eugene) with Helmuth Rilling conducting.

Krzysztof Penderecki launched his career as a conductor in 1972. In the past twenty–five years he has conducted most of the world's greatest orchestras, including the Berlin Philharmonic Orchestra, Munich Philharmonic Orchestra, The Norddeutscher Runkfunk Orchestra (Hamburg), the Mitteldeutscher Rundfunk Sinfonie Orchester (Leipzig), the NHK Orchestra (Tokyo), the Osaka Philharmonic, the London Symphony, the New York Philharmonic, the Philadelphia Orchestra, and Sinfonia Varsovia. He has been artistic director of the Casals Festival in San Juan, Puerto Rico, since 1993.

As a teacher, Krzysztof Penderecki is associated above all with his alma mater, the Academy of Music in Cracow (where he has been professor since 1958 and where he served as Rector from 1972–87). He was a lecturer at the Volkwang Hochschule für Musik in Essen from 1966–68 and professor at the Yale University School of Music from 1972–78.

He is a member of the Royal Academy of Music in London, the Akademie der Künste in Berlin, the Academia Nacional de Bellas Artes in Buenos Aires, the Académie Internationale de Philosophie et de l'Art in Berne, the Polish Academy of Learning and the Royal Irish Academy of Music in Dublin. Krzysztof Penderecki has won numerous awards, including the Medici Prize, the Sibelius Prize, the Herder Prize, the Jurzykowski Prize, the Grawemeyer Award and the Karl Wolf Israel Foundation Prize. He has also received honorary doctorates from many universities, including those of Rochester, Leuven, Bordeaux, Georgetown, Belgrade, Poznań, Warsaw and Glasgow,

Krzysztof Penderecki lives in Cracow and Lusławice, Poland, and in Lucerne, Switzerland.